THE ICONOCLAST'S
—— GUIDE TO ——
FOODIES

DOG 'n' BONE

THE ICONOCLAST'S

— GUIDE TO —

FOODIES

UNRAVELING THE MINDSET OF A FOOD SNOB IN 50 DIGESTIBLE CHUNKS

ALEXANDRA PARSONS

DOG 'N' BONE

Published in 2012 by Dog 'n' Bone Books
An imprint of Ryland Peters & Small Ltd
20–21 Jockey's Fields   519 Broadway, 5th Floor
London WC1R 4BW   New York, NY 10012

www.dogandbonebooks.com

10 9 8 7 6 5 4 3 2 1

Text © Alexandra Parsons 2012
Design and photography © Dog 'n' Bone Books 2012

A CIP catalog record for this book is available from the Library of Congress and the British Library.

ISBN: 978 0 957140 91 2

Printed in China

Editor: Caroline West
Design: Wide Open Design
Illustration: Steve Millington aka Lord Dunsby

For digital editions, visit www.cicobooks.com/apps.php

Contents

CHAPTER 1
The Foodie Cooks

Cutlery—You Are
  What You Eat With   12
Strangely Shaped Plates   14
The Salad Olympics   16
Irony Food   18
He'll Be With Us Shortly   20
It Is Possible to Know Too
  Much About Stuff   22
Incident With a Blowtorch   24
Chemistry Set Cooking   26
Home With the Range   28
Themed Cheese   30
The Beach Barbecue   32
Déjeuner Sur L'Herbe   34
Goose Up Christmas   36

CHAPTER 2
In the Foodie Kitchen

The Slaughter of the Innocents   40
Guts 'n' Gore   42
Extreme Fish   44
The Seasonal Slave   46
Give Us Our Daily   48
Can and Can't   50
Chili Bore   52
Coffee—Not As Simple As
  You Think   54
The Tea Ceremony   56
The Ages of Vinegar   58
The Chastity of Olive Oil   60
The Sun-Dried Tomato   62
Salt   64
The Truffle Shaver   66
Wine Gift Overload   68

CHAPTER 3
The Foodie Out and About

Adventures With Wine   72
The Language of Wine   74
Market Day   76
Three-Star Dining   78
Lovingly Hand-Written in *Jus*   80
Your Usual Table   82
I'll Order For You, Shall I?   84
Nigel@foodieblog.com   88
The Pop Up   91
Adventurous Eating
  to No Purpose   94
On the Ethnic Trail   96

CHAPTER 4
The Foodie Lifestyle

What Foodies Read   100
Foodie Myths   102
Foodie Baby Names   104
Cheesy Baby Names   109
Raising a Foodie   112
Worship the Food   114
Foodie Movie Moments   116
Foodie Music   118
Foodie Games   120
Going For a Walk—
  Coming Back With Lunch   122
Don't Get Too Fond of Flopsy   124

Index   126
Acknowledgments   128

Introduction

Just so you know where I'm coming from: I love food. I like to cook. I like it when people cook for me. I look forward to every meal. I like a well-presented plate as much as anyone. I enjoy good conversation around a dining table and I like eating spaces to be pleasant and practical. I am basically all in favor of foodies and "foodie-ism" if it means better food on my plain, white, round plate. But foodies always want to go further—and further—and, as the purpose of this book is to stamp out pretentious foodie crimes, let us begin with two of my pet hates.

Over-decorated tables
While not strictly a foodie flaw—because the food doesn't really figure—this is competitive dining at its worst. I have sat

at a dining table so artfully laden with blossoms, trinkets, centerpieces, and witty, twiddly touches that fellow diners were rendered invisible, the pleated silk napkins were impossible to release from their restraining twists of ivy, and the wine in gilded, colored-glass goblets was difficult to

appreciate. Fun factor? Round about zero. Try and imagine an evening spent shouting over a barrage of delphiniums, eyes streaming with hay fever, and all conversation reduced to variations on the theme of the hostess, her beautiful home, and her impeccable taste.

Invisible vegetables
Food that has been teased into towers, decorated with amusing blobs and arty smears usually comes with an "impression" of vegetables on the plate. I do not call a small, perfectly formed "vegetablette" that has been fashioned out of a larger vegetable anything other than a waste of time and vegetables. And, if you are going to give me spinach, then give me some spinach I can see.

Now that I've got that off my chest, what follows is an affectionate poke in the foodie ribs; not a declaration of war—except against spun-sugar swans, flowers carved from radishes, and those jaunty, eye-gouging decorative spears of deep-fried spaghetti.

CHAPTER 1
The Foodie Cooks

Cutlery—You Are What You Eat With

Knives and forks need to be a bit hefty. You need to invest in quality and design, and I do sympathize with the foodie who takes his eating irons seriously. You need nicely balanced implements and the security that comes from knowing your fork will not bend when you spear a roast potato with enthusiasm. And I also think you need steak knives. But, that said, things can get wildly out of control in the cutlery drawer, especially for the more traditional foodie who has inherited massive canteens of silverware from great-aunts or who takes delight in shopping for antique jelly spoons, caviar spoons, egg spoons, and runcible spoons; pickle forks, fish forks and fondue forks; butter knives, fruit knives, and grapefruit knives. Of course, it is delightful to eat your asparagus with an asparagus fork and to spoon up every last drop of gravy—sorry, *jus* —with a *saucier* spoon but it is, frankly, unnecessary.

For normal people, laying the table means finding a matching knife and fork, maybe a spoon for the pudding, a napkin, and a glass, but for the obsessive foodie, putting cutlery on the table is an art in itself: knives, forks, and spoons arranged in course order (working from the outside in), edges of the cutlery lined up precisely two fingers' width from the edge of the table—a method he'll have picked up from watching butlers at work in period dramas.

I don't quite know if the cutlery drawer can rise to the challenge of the 11 or 12 course tasting dinner—each place setting would have to be a good few yards long, but perhaps this is the moment to think about multi-use utensils such as the spork, the spife, the knork, and the sporf. I leave you to imagine their function. Meanwhile, may I suggest a gift item guaranteed to really, really upset the serious foodie: an embarrassing, battery-powered spaghetti fork that twizzles at the touch of a button, spraying Bolognese sauce over the astonished company. A tease at 5.99 from Amazon.

Fig. 1
No wonder they invented the knork

Strangely
Shaped Plates

Blame Japanese restaurants for serving beautiful, tasty morsels
of food on exquisite slivers of interesting porcelain in a very
experience-enhancing way. Then, along comes fine dining and
suddenly round plates with a rim just aren't good enough any
more. Not enough space to show off the towers of invention
and the artistic trail of colorful blobs that replace gravy in
these times.

So we get long, thin, rectangular plates, perfect for anything
long and thin like a leek or a solitary stick of celery; fish-shaped
plates (the perfect choice for fish, obviously); and octagonal
plates (so handy for octopus). The choice is daunting: oval plates,
asymmetrical plates, and S-shaped curves, which must work for
something if only to distract attention from how little food there
is on the plate. But some are beautiful objects to behold. Take,
for instance, the special risotto bowl with a big, flat rim and
a little depression that really draws attention to the contents...
once you've experienced that, a blob of risotto in an ordinary
bowl just doesn't cut it. The more the foodie thinks about it, the
clearer it becomes that a set of six, eight, or maybe 12 is needed!
And the foodie must have several sets of square plates that won't
fit in the dishwasher because they look so stylish and, according
to feng shui principles, square plates are grounding and will
slow you down.

Now comes the issue of storage because what you may fail
to realize in the heat of the acquisition moment is that a lot
of these fancy shapes don't stack. So, with every available

cupboard filling up fast with teetering piles of oval platters, boat-shaped bowls, and daring ellipses of all kinds, plus a set of chunky, wooden steak boards and those must-have slabs of slate, some sort of system has to be devised. There is little point in having octopus plates if you can't find them when you need them. So, there's a foodie task for a long winter's night: a Plate Organization, Classification, and Retrieval System. Enjoy!

Fig. 2

To hell with Robbie Burns, we need room for the haggis plates

The Salad Olympics

Just a simple green salad? Dream on. For a foodie, salads are a category of Olympic competition. The baby leaves, specially selected, lovingly washed, and individually dried are only the beginning—balances of taste must be created between bitter and sweet, crunchy and soft, while contrasts of color must be chosen from the bright green, the dark green, the red, and the purple. And there has to be something surprising to catch the judge's eye and palate while being careful to remain within category—

*Fig.*3
And the winner is...

will that nasturtium prove to be a disqualifier? The bowl has to be large enough to do justice to the tossing section of the competition, but small enough to present the leaves in an enticing pile. The dressing has taken weeks of measuring, shaking, and seasoning, while the choice of oil has had him tossing and turning in his sleep for a week before the big day. Has he done enough? Will other contestants cheat? Should he cheat? Could he somehow impregnate the bowl with essence of crispy bacon?

Nothing if not versatile, his main-course salad is also a contender. Every ingredient, from the soft-poached quail's eggs to the delicate slivers of peeled and de-seeded tomatoes, the toasted pine nuts, and the fillets of Cantabrian anchovy, has been sourced from saintly and patient suppliers who finally turned off their phones when his name came up on screen. He baked several batches of bread to create the perfect crouton, and bought 20 bunches of herbs to pick the most perfect leaves to top his creation.

Come the big day, the foodie is a bundle of nerves, his hand shaking the dressing bottle clawed with tension. At the assembly point, other contestants nonchalantly place their contributions to the feast on the table and wander off to the refreshment zone. The foodie, concerned his tomatoes are watery and his pea shoots are limp, is frozen to the spot.

"Please, Bernard," his wife mutters through clenched teeth. "It's a party. Lighten up! They only asked you to bring a couple of salads. It's no big deal!"

Irony Food

Such a good foodie joke, isn't it? Poking fun at the common and the kitsch, and giving it a boost of foodie know-how? That's why people will stand in a queue for hours to be allowed into a crowded pop-up restaurant in an abandoned warehouse to eat gourmet hamburgers in buns, and why we are delighted to be offered teeny tiny hot dogs with mustard and minuscule paper cones of fish and chips while mingling with fellow sophisticates at cocktail parties. And that's how the seafood cocktail and the Black Forest gâteau have wormed their way back on the menu. They've been "foodied." Inspired by the trend, our foodie has

Fig. 4
Bean there, done that!

just got to have a go at an "*homage soirée*" because even foodies have a sense of humor. He is going to tackle a typically British, 1970s nostalgia menu that was once the height of sophistication: Seafood Cocktail, Steak with Mushrooms, followed by Black Forest Gâteau from the dessert trolley. He's keeping back the retro American menu of Grapefruit and Avocado Salad Mold, Chicken à la King (with the sauce courtesy of Campbell's condensed mushroom soup), and Strawberry Shortcake swished down with a glass of Tang, until he can devise a foodie way of replicating a sweetened drink powder artificially colored and flavored orange.

The original shrimp cocktail made from limp, defrosted shrimp and tasteless lettuce, and then smothered with creamy gloop from a jar, now zings upon the palate with freshly cooked seafood, interesting, crunchy salad leaves, and a masterly mayonnaise. The steak served well done, back in the '70s, is rare and juicy in this updated version, while the mushrooms are earthy little girolles tossed in garlic and parsley. The Black Forest Gâteau, like the Strawberry Shortcake, used to be manufactured by the thousand in industrial parks up and down the country, using ingredients from a laboratory and an aerosol. What were they thinking of? The foodie has been baking since dawn and produced a moist, rich, and booze-laden mouthful of wonderfulness and, by the flickering light of candles stuck in straw-wrapped Chianti bottles, we've all been made to eat our scorn and be grateful we live in foodie times.

He'll Be With Us Shortly

Or will he? When the foodie entertains, it is a very serious business. Either he has spent a week reducing stock, sourcing free-range ptarmigans, clarifying aspic, and generally going for his fine-dining Masterchef badge, or he's going to throw it all together at the last minute using unusual ingredients picked up at the market from which he will confidently produce something spontaneously different. Either way, ensuring his guests have a pleasant, relaxing evening is not top of his agenda. The food is top of his agenda, even if it means absenting himself for long periods to nurture soufflés, gut fish, or poach brains. The assembled company are left to chat among themselves and nervously wonder if they are going to be "challenged" into eating something weird.

I vaguely knew such a foodie once upon a time, and I offer this as a cautionary tale. I think the foodie in question had actually run out of real friends who would accept invitations to dine. I was rail-roaded into going by a friend who had been similarly rail-roaded, and then neither of them turned up. So, picture a very hesitant group with nothing in common and no host. We did learn that he had been in the garage all afternoon with a hairdryer and some ducks, but beyond that there was no hint of what to expect. There was a distracted girlfriend who appeared fleetingly, but never sat down and didn't know anybody either. There was wine on the table but no implements with which to open it. Whenever the girlfriend left us, sounds of a pitched battle filtered through from the kitchen.

The Foodie Cooks

Finally, the host appeared with a bad cut over his left eye and two perfect, gleaming, mahogany-dark, roasted Peking ducks; he mumbled a brief "hello" and that was the last we ever saw of him. The girlfriend wandered in and out with things in bowls and then started the painful procession of pancake delivery— just two at a time because, of course, each pancake was being made from scratch and he only had two pancake pans. However, friendships were forged under fire. One guest attacked the duck with a serving spoon and another found a corkscrew in her handbag. I think it might have been me. A memorable evening, but not in a good way.

Fig. 5
Alone in the garage with duck and hairdryer. Meanwhile…

It Is Possible to Know Too Much About Stuff

You've been offered this enormous green olive. It's not something you can nonchalantly pop in your mouth—as you carry on chatting over pre-dinner drinks—so, you've got to put down the glass of bio-dynamic, organic *Conegliano-Valdobbiadene Prosecco* you were so enjoying (in spite of the lecture you've just had about the residual sugar levels and how the base wine is re-fermented in pressurized tanks and is designed to be drunk young), take the beast in both hands, and nibble the flesh off the pit as if it were a chicken leg. Your foodie host is eyeballing you disconcertingly, waiting for a reaction.

"It's nice," you smile when you've finally swallowed. But you are wondering if you'll have any appetite left for dinner.

"NICE! Listen, do you know what you've just eaten? That was an authentic, artisanal *Bella di Cerignola* olive imported directly from the Fratepietro farm in Puglia! Meaty, ripe, delicate, and sweet! So delicate, in fact, that they have to be picked individually by hand and stored in padded boxes! Here, let me pass you the pistachios: the Long Akbari variety from Iran, naturally—the best in my opinion. Classified, you know, by the shape of the kernel…"

As your host drivels on, you realize he is determined to share every last fact with you and that this dinner, although undoubtedly delicious, is going to be a nightmare given that you're only on the nibbles. All attempts to swing the conversation round to house prices, religion, or breast implants have so far failed. Have a fit and call a cab.

Fig. 6

"Quick! Before he starts on the genealogy of the grouse"

It is Possible to Know Too Much About Stuff

Incident With a Blowtorch

Alarming noises coming from the kitchen? Smoke alarm disabled? It is safe to assume that the foodie has acquired a blowtorch.

All normal meal preparation is suspended while the foodie gets to grips with this new gadget: breakfast is burnt toast and blow-torched bananas followed by a snack of caramelized meringues and toasted marshmallows. The kitchen resembles a war zone with buckled baking trays cooling in the sink and dish cloths with jagged holes and burn marks draped over melting chopping boards. It is a learning curve. Lunch? Blasted cheese toasts on top of onion soup—actually, that does sound rather good. Tea-time with bruléed cream cake? Different, not quite Baked Alaska but you can see where he's going with this. Surely sanity will creep back round about suppertime? Sorry, but no. He's ditched the puny kitchen blowtorch in favor of a heavy-duty DIY model and is planning to seriously blacken a couple of steaks, maybe crisp up a chicken, and blast-roast a couple of peppers.

Back at the DIY store, the foodie has gone macho and is looking for inspiration in the aisles. A circular saw for shredding cabbage? Extreme carving? A sanding machine for speed-grating Parmesan, yes! Ditch that namby-pamby palette knife for a plasterer's trowel. An electric drill with all the bits: perfect for precision studding a roast with garlic, pitting cherries, and coring apples.

Why has no one thought of it before? A sledgehammer! Brilliant! All tenderizing needs met with one swift blow and a magic way to purée an apple. Easy, tiger!

Fig. 7
"That's the toast done, now for the scrambled eggs"

Chemistry Set Cooking

Syringe, pipette, nitrous oxide, carboxymethyl cellulose, and sodium alginate...what do they remind you of? Dozing off at the back of Mr. Harbottle's chemistry class? Snappy dialog from a movie set in an embalming parlor? You'd be wrong. Welcome to the world of molecular gastronomy, from which there is probably no escape. Now that the foodie has bought his first Introductory Kit, no ingredient is safe from his foaming, gelling, and spherification experiments. Oh do keep up! His kitchen resembles the bridge of the Starship Enterprise and the larder is filling up with alarming little packets of white powder with scientific names. He is in a high state of excitement because a fellow "moleculer" has just texted to say that supplies of Kappa Carrageenan have just landed from a galaxy somewhere beyond the Milky Way, and Trevor from work has succeeded in "globulizing" a turnip.

It's lunchtime, and people need to be fed. But there's a block of dry ice fizzing and smoking malevolently where the toaster used to be, and the foodie's too busy changing the cartridges in his gas gun to bother with a tiresome concept like lunch. An egg would be nice, but all the eggs have been emptied out and re-filled with Parmesan and prosciutto ice cream and what were tomatoes are now a six-foot long jellified noodle.

How about heating up some soup? It would seem simple enough, but nothing is simple in this brave new world. "Heat" requires molecular friction, thermometers, and pressure gauges, plus the equipment needs to be re-calibrated. Soup? That's not soup! It is carrots and fresh tarragon in liquid form that will be powdered, emulsified, turned into a balloon, and filled with mozzarella. This is the moment to step into the handy Hadron collider he has assembled in the back yard to vaporize peas, press a few buttons, pull a few levers, and get yourself sent back to last week to intercept the mailman with that special-offer Molecular Starter Kit.

Fig. 8

"Honey, I dry-iced the dog!"

Home With the Range

Fig. 9

...where the deer and the antelope roast...

The Aga. A statement oven that roasts, toasts, irons sheets, heats the house, supplies endless hot water, warms the dog, breaks the bank with fuel costs, and CAN NEVER BE TURNED OFF except when it goes wrong and then it CAN NEVER BE TURNED BACK ON. The foodie is tempted by the bucolic delights of joining the charmed Aga Circle, learning its secret language and investing in its unique range of roasting pans and casseroles. Happy memories of weekends with country foodies have affected his judgement: a joint of pork cooking to crackling perfection through the night and perfuming the whole house; cozy, toasty, eggy breakfasts; warm socks; crusty loaves; and returning to an Aga-warm welcome after a damp hike through bosky woods in search of mushrooms. He dreams of dense fruit cakes gently baking away while he's potting up his pickles; of *dauphinoise* potatoes, effortlessly making themselves creamy on the inside and crunchy on top while he's out blasting away at pheasants in the fresh country air.

Time for the country foodie to 'fess up to the disasters that can befall an Aga-dependent home with no back-up facilities. The desperate searches for Aga technicians in the night, the ruinous cost of replacement thermo-couplers, and Mark One burners. Days with no hot water, no heat, and no hot food. Then try summer time with an Aga. Many Aga-lovers are forced to leave home and find a summer rental at the beach. But does all that matter when you can simmer stockpots through the night? Dry herbs in pretty bunches? Rescue little orphaned lambs?

Even the smitten foodie is beginning to acknowledge that Agas belong in large, stone-flagged country houses with larders full of game and 4x4s parked in the driveway—definitely not in the life of an urban foodie with a small kitchen, a day job, and a tiny Toyota in the residents' parking bay. In another life, maybe.

Themed Cheese

How does the foodie stay ahead of the game with his cheeseboard? A theme always goes down well. One route is to go for an Animal of Origin theme: a sheep's cheese selection, a goat's cheese, a cow, or a buffalo, and that (unless some rival foodie has found an enthusiastic cheese-maker who has been milking ants or giraffes) should give plenty of scope.

Country of Origin: that's another good, reliable theme. French cheeses: you feel the French kind of invented cheese and in their enthusiasm have produced at least 1,000 varieties, so the foodie is bound to find three or four that no one has ever heard of before. Italian cheeses: plenty of very obscure stuff from artisan producers that will get the foodie going, but even the mainstream seduces—who could fail to fall for the charms of a creamy Dolcelatte and a hunk of proper Parmesan? British cheeses are excellent, diverse, and full of personality. Dutch and Belgian cheeses are also worthy, but just a bit dull. So far, so predictable. Out there on the foodie edge, finding a decent selection of Norwegian cheese could be a challenge. Chinese cheese is probably rubbish, but it would be a real mission to source. Indian cheese has few fans outside the Indian community and Middle Eastern cheese, like the politics, is unpredictable and confusing. Latvian cheese is frankly not worth the effort.

The more perverse foodie might go for an Age-range theme: a young and soft, a middle-aged stinker, and a gnarled vintage number that requires an ice pick to get through the rind. Or how about an Alphabet theme: just pick a letter and go for it. As a concept it requires a lot of explaining, giving the foodie ample opportunity to show off and bask in admiration for his oh-so-witty way with food. Don't forget, you read about it here first: Brie, Bergkase, Brynza, Buxton Blue...

Final suggestion is The Irony Board: a tub of Philadelphia cream cheese, seal insouciantly folded back halfway, a chunk of processed cheddar, and a slightly slimy Danish Blue served up with sticks of celery and salty crackers. It would be a brave foodie whose reputation could survive that one.

Fig.10

"I know I'll be hungry again in an hour, but..."

The Beach Barbecue

Ingredients for a normal barbecue on the beach: a modest grill,
a bag of charcoal, a pack of burgers, some interesting, marinated
chicken drumsticks, bread, a bowl of salad, a squeezy bottle
of tomato ketchup, and some bananas to grill for pudding.
Conveniently, it all fits neatly in the back of the car alongside
the beach volleyball, the rugs, and the beer.

A bit further down the beach from this delightful set-up with its
filmic qualities of harmony and good times a-coming, the foodie

Fig. 11

"It'll make a great breakfast, guys!"

The Foodie Cooks

has set out his pitch. He arrived at dawn to dig the hole, and has been working ever since. He's manhandled half a hundredweight of stones to line his pit, gathered driftwood for the fire he has nurtured all morning, and is waiting for the rocks to get hot. He's dirty and sweaty, smudged with ash, and his fringe is singed. It seems so simple in the movies. "Hey! Let's BBQ!" The juvenile lead and his buddies, all tan and teeth, flurry about in the sand without breaking sweat, and in the next frame, girls in bikinis are nibbling corn-cobs, sucking lobster claws, and smiling with promise.

No such luck here. The foodie is already getting pretty snippy with his mates who seem to think all they have to do is pitch up, chat to each other, and crack open the beer. But he's got to roll up his chinos and paddle in the shallows collecting seaweed; huff and puff it back to the pit; and then distribute all his lovingly foil-wrapped parcels of clams, mussels, potatoes, onions, and whatever in the smoking seaweed. Then, it's more seaweed and a whole heap of heavy, stinky, seaweed-soaked sacking to wrestle with.

Now comes the interminable wait, hoping he's not overdone it with the sea water and extinguished the embers. Time to worry about serving iced soup and chilled chardonnay from coolers that are draining his car battery, maybe thinking he could have asked for help even though he's convinced building a barbecue pit is not a job for frivolous amateurs. Of course, the food— when it comes—will be a triumph and the experience totally memorable, but consider an alternative ending: the gathering clouds darken, the temperature drops, fat summer raindrops first spatter and then hammer down. The crowd up the beach have already enjoyed their simple lunch, lobbed their stuff in the car, and headed home. So, here's the big dilemma: do you leave the clams for someone else to dig up, or wait it out?

Déjeuner Sur L'Herbe

The foodie and two of his oldest friends are meeting up for a classic picnic, and I think you can safely say that our foodie has surpassed himself with a mere two days of preparation. He's poached eggs in red wine with strips of bacon and baby onions, and nestled them in little china bowls. He's roasted a pheasant, jointed it, skinned it, boned it, and trimmed it; prepared a flavorsome sauce with game stock and truffles; and chilled his pheasant pieces on a rack, poured over his sauce—oh so carefully—and chilled them some more. Then he's adorned his *chaud-froid* of pheasant with decorative truffle cut-outs, carroty fronds, and tarragon leaves, and he's coated them all in an aspic flavored with Madeira and truffle jus. They look old-school-amazing. He's knocked up a little salad of seasonal baby leaves and poured a stunning, mustardy vinaigrette into a little screw-top jar. Freshly laundered napkins, decent cutlery, vintage Bakelite plates, and proper glasses are packed into his picnic hamper along with a freshly baked loaf of wholemeal bread wrapped in a brand-new linen cloth and a proper picnic rug with a waterproof bottom.

Arriving at the picnic spot, he sees his mate Jonny Dash has got there first. Jonny's sitting on a tree stump, rummaging in a plastic bag: "Now what have I got here—cheese sandwiches, yup! Pickled onions, natch! Couple of bottles of brown ale. Can't go wrong with that, mate." And here comes the third member of the party, lolloping across the field with a cheery smile and what looks like a dog's blanket thrown over one shoulder. It's Peregrine Posh, and from his battered, old school satchel he produces a game pie from Fortnum and Mason's and a bottle of his wine merchant's best claret. It's a feast, of course, and our foodie can't help but feel a trifle superior, which was the whole point of the exercise. But on the other hand...the cheese was an amazing vintage cheddar, the game pie was a knockout, and both Peregrine and Jonny felt they'd taught their foodie friend an interesting little lesson.

Fig. 12

Dedicated foodies still determined to ignore the beauties of nature

Goose Up Christmas

The foodie has finally wrested control of Christmas from the iron grip of the in-laws and the aunts. This festive season is his moment to shine. Nothing he can do about the guest list, however, as the aunts are a traditional fixture and they have expectations. Once they have put on their party hats and downed something sparkling, the aunts will be expecting a starter of smoked salmon. After a small pause and some risqué reminiscences from Aunt Angelica about her misspent youth, a massive, gleaming turkey will appear at the table and Grandpa will carve—badly, but generously. There will be handfuls of solid chestnut stuffing, a vast dish of slightly overdone Brussels sprouts, a rustling pile of roast potatoes (which will have gone cold by the time Grandpa's done with the massacre, but then redeemed by jugfuls of hot gravy), and pretty dishes of cranberry sauce with silver spoons. Once second and third helpings are out of the way, it is time for one of the children to throw a carbohydrate-induced tantrum, and Aunt Angelica to fall asleep quite gracefully with her head resting comfortably on her plate, still clutching on to her glass. A dimming of lights and it is time for the well-rehearsed drama of a flaming Christmas pudding and a very stiff black coffee for Aunt Angelica. All in all, a tried-and-tested formula that rekindles family bonds and pleases all, washed down with copious amounts of red wine. (Rather too copious for some, perhaps, not naming any names.)

But this year, it is different. There is champagne, but it comes with a rather boring lecture about provenance and, frankly, there's not enough of it. The Christmas party shuffle to their seats and settle in front of the starter, anticipating moist mats of pink fish, slices of thin-cut brown bread, and a wedge of lemon, but are confronted by a tiny, trembling tower of squid and chorizo. Barely a mouthful! Then, after an interminable wait (during which the children set fire to the dog and Aunt Angelica moves from misspent youth to the murkier waters of The Second Divorce), a hot and bothered foodie delivers each guest a huge plate with a few slivers of goose, a dribble of *jus*, a thimbleful of sage-and-onion stuffing, a shredded leaf of *cavolo nero*, and a single roast potato that looks like a hedgehog. We won't go into the pudding, but it featured neither brandy nor flames, and it did not go down well. It's nice to do something different for Christmas! But why? Why bother messing with something that works?

Fig. 13

"Excuse me, dear, but if that's Christmas dinner, then I'm Brigitte Bardot"

CHAPTER 2
In the Foodie Kitchen

The Slaughter of the Innocents

Cabbages the diameter of a golf ball, carrots and baby corn no bigger than a toddler's little finger? It doesn't seem right, does it, uprooting young vegetables barely out of seedling-hood? A carrot needs some time in the ground to taste carroty, a zucchini needs to live a little to acquire character and, as for the eggplant, well, there is no real point to an eggplant if it can't pick up flavors from nearby, and that's a skill that takes a bit of time to learn—young eggplants need to hang out with their roots for a while to get with the vibe. And, speaking of size, could someone please tell me what to do with a cauliflower the size of an olive? How many would you need to make cauliflower cheese, a decent curry, or that earthy spaghetti sauce with garlic and anchovies? Basically, what's the point of the thing?

Oops, here comes the foodie with a special delivery of embryonic micro-vegetables—and a plan. He's going to poach or maybe roast his mini nursery and present it as a colorful medley on a lovely sculptural platter decorated with baby herbs that have been snipped off with nail scissors before they've had a chance to feel the sun on their leaves—very eye-catching. Pretty as a picture, in fact. A mini grocery store's window display from a children's toy store. And, of course, everyone is doing it. Teenage vegetables are *sooo* last year. Which begs the question: given this slaughter of the innocents to feed the latest foodie frenzy, will any vegetables be allowed to grow up ever again? We'll be left explaining to our grandchildren that once upon a time you could make a glorious dish of sweet-and-sour red cabbage from shredding just the one. Now that they're the size of marbles, it takes 106.

Fig. 14

"Do tell me, what will this grow up to be? A carrot?"

Guts 'n' Gore

Vegetarians should look away now. There are bits of animal that everyone eats: shoulders, legs, rumps, and loins, and these are eaten because they are tender and tasty, not too fatty, and quite easy to cook. And there are bits of animal that only the foodie craves: tails, necks, heads, feet, tummies, and intimate body parts. This is not just because they are plain weird and most people consider them best recycled as pet food, but because they represent a real challenge to the cook, create a *frisson* on the palate, and allow the foodie to describe elaborately the efforts he has been to in order to test the mettle and stomach of his guests. Why? Because that's what foodies do.

At the time of writing, the average butcher does not display such things, but in remoter areas of the globe (where women still dress in black and wear aprons all day long), you can still see butchers' windows that look more like a mortuary scene from a gory thriller, with slimy things in stainless-steel bins, as well as gruesome piles of glands decorated with sprigs of parsley and roses made out of carrots. This is foodie heaven. The foodie will be sniffing and prodding, and trying out deficient language skills on the baffled natives, as he selects chicken feet, pituitary glands, a heart-and-lung combo, an ear, and a bucket of blood for a dish described in a cookery book three centuries old and written in Latin.

Unfortunately, it's a foodie trend. So, beware...the day will come when a supermarket near you opens up a "Guts 'n' Gore" counter, and that will be the time to refuse invitations from your foodie friends for an "interesting" dining experience.

Fig. 15

It takes a certain kind of person to relish the truly intimate parts of an animal...

Extreme Fish

Browsing at the fish store for anything unfamiliar or poking about the discards stuck in the nets on the quayside, the foodie is after something different. Ah, here we go, an ugly jumble of gray, slithery stuff with suckers! Brilliant. It's a giant squid—well, there's more than one website devoted to unsuccessful ways to make that edible, from soaking it overnight in milk to throwing it straight in the back of a garbage truck. So, good luck with that.

And, passing over the familiar delights of oysters, mussels, and clams, here's a pile of really uncompromising molluscs— abalone, jumbo whelks, and conch—so tough they have to be tenderized with repeated blows from a blunt instrument and tasting so rubbery that they have to be drowned in garlic and chili. So, there you have it: rising to challenges set by the tough, the bad, and the downright tasteless of the deep, the foodie is off once again on a voyage of discovery with his pan and a slice of lemon, pausing only to harvest sea urchins from a handy rock pool and risking injury from poisonous spines to slurp out the coral there and then. (We did enjoy the uncertainty of that moment, but put the show-off outcome down to luck rather than good judgement.)

So, he's got to try fugu, hasn't he? That Japanese blowfish experience "for the adventurous of spirit." With a liver containing a poison 1,200 times more deadly than cyanide (never mind the other deadly organs), the fugu is fiendishly tricky to prepare — special fugu chefs devote whole careers to it and still people die, while a lot more get very sick and very frightened. But what does it taste like? Opinions vary from "fairly pleasant" and "probably an acquired taste" to "bland and boring." It lives in brackish waters and has an unpleasant, vindictive nature, so how can it possibly taste good? And the experience? Well, that rates from adrenalin-pumping to near-death, remembering that the slight tingle on the lips is from the toxic tetrodotoxin for which there is no cure. So, how lucky do you feel, foodie?

Fig. 16

*Spot the unpleasant item with a
vindictive nature and a death wish*

The Seasonal Slave

The foodie is on pretty solid ground here. No one could argue that eating seasonally is a bad thing. We should all be doing it: looking forward to the strawberry season, enjoying ripe tomatoes and heat rashes at the height of summer, and plucking game birds from the larder when the nights draw in and the ski season beckons. But you know the foodie is going to take this to extremes. There'll be no sneaky pack of frozen peas in the freezer, no apple tarts in August, and no tomato salad with your Turkey leftovers.

The foodie year will be a fixed round. January is for root vegetables, cabbages, and maybe a wild duck. February: hurrah! A rabbit, venison stew, more cabbages, a dozen oysters, and some early forced rhubarb. March: broccoli (don't all rush at once), wild salmon, and beets. April: spring lamb, new potatoes, proper rhubarb and, don't panic, there's enough broccoli for everyone. May: asparagus—yes! But broccoli is still around and so is rhubarb. June: strawberries and cherries are the highlights, but there's still some rhubarb left, so don't worry. July: salad, at last! And peas and more strawberries, please. August: tomatoes—can hardly wait! Cherries, berries, and plums, and we've still got salad, so that's good. September: shrimp, salmon, celery, game birds, and nuts. October: thankfully, it's the start of the cabbage season (we were missing it a bit there), plus pheasants and partridges, apples and onions, and pumpkins for Hallowe'en. November: haddock and herrings, a few game birds are still about, as are Brussels sprouts and, of course, cabbage. December: fields of turkeys and geese looking a bit nervous, plenty of game, more nuts, a glut of Brussels sprouts, and, I know you'll be thrilled to hear it, many varieties of cabbage.

No wonder mankind invented airfreight, polytunnels, and freezers; otherwise the poor Mediterranean foodie would be staring glumly at a vast pile of rotting oranges, lemons, peaches, figs, and olives, and we'd never be able to share our glorious bounty of rhubarb, cabbages, and broccoli with the world.

Fig. 17
Cabbage mille feuille, anyone?

Give Us Our Daily

Flour, water, a bit of yeast, a pinch of salt, mix it up, thrash it about a bit, and stick it in the oven. Made for centuries along basically the same lines, bread is a staple food in almost all cultures and every sane person who is not beset with gluten allergies or fussing about on a carb-free diet loves it. Just a thought...historically, people ate vast quantities of bread, the rich ate massive, meaty meals off a huge slice of it, and the poor got the slice and a bit of gruel to dip it in. So, what happened to medieval peasants with gluten allergies? Got all bloated and died, I guess. And there's no denying that Henry VIII would have benefited from a carb-free diet...so, yes, bread has a downside after all.

But I digress. Once you get all foodie about bread, life's less simple. You can only bake and eat so much (see above), but, if you choose to get precious and have a bread for every culinary moment, there'll be about 20 loaves on the go in just the one household, and not much storage space left for the pâté that makes snack-time toast irresistible, the goat's cheese to spread on that crusty baguette, the smoked salmon and cream cheese that go on the bagel, the olive oil to dip your focaccia into, the hummus to spread onto your pitta bread, or the refried beans to stuff into your tortilla. And, remember, that lot are on the lower slopes of foodieness. A real breadie will want to try a Roquefort and almond sourdough that costs as much as filet mignon, but is, of course, exquisite. And why stop there? Pondering how to serve the cheese, the foodie will go for a loaf made with spring water and organic spelt flour that takes two days to make and comes in its own presentation box. Divine, I'm sure, but the morning after it'll be stale.

Fig.18

5,000 loaves and no fishes

Can and Can't

How shocking to discover that in the foodie's larder—among the myriad flours and sugars, the 17 different types of rice, and the sack of cornmeal lugged back as extortionately expensive baggage on a cheap flight from Genoa—are TIN CANS! Convenience foods—whatever next? Canned tomatoes, yes, but they're not from the supermarket. They're organically grown, hand-picked, steam-peeled, and packed into snug-fitting cans with organic basil and a touch of sea salt—and then shipped in from California. Highly convenient, I think you'll agree.

And there are also cans of anchovies, but not as we know them because these cans of *Boquerones* (which as any fool knows are marinated in white vinegar and taste quite nasty in a Cesar salad) and *Anchoias* (the dark, salty ones preserved in the most virgin of olive oils) have been packed in fancy, colorful cans and imported from Spain, while the stash of *sardine* comes from Portugal. There are a lot of canned beans in there: garbanzo beans, lima beans, pinto beans, cranberry beans, turtle beans, and navy beans, all organically grown, packed without salt, and acquired via obscure websites from fellow obsessives. But here's an altogether different type of bean—packed in a familiar blue tin with white writing proclaiming the brand name of a certain Mr. Henry John Heinz. How did that get past the censor? Our foodie is not a fool. Gently warmed through with a dash of Angostura bitters and decanted onto sourdough toast slicked with salted butter from Normandy, she calls it *Bruschetta con Fagioli Stufati*. We call it baked-beans-on-toast heaven.

Fig.19
"300 cans of sardines – for your own use?"

Chili Bore

For the average cook there is a choice of mild, medium, or hot powders; for the more adventurous, the evil-looking pack of chili flakes or the randomly labeled, fresh chili peppers in the supermarket vegetable section. But for the chili bore, there is a world of obscure stuff in Scoville Heat Scale land that no one wants to know about and an infinite number of specialty suppliers who have dedicated their lives to the cultivation of ever-hotter varieties of the genus *Capsicum*. And yes! There are chili festivals and chili cook-offs galore. You can make a whole bunch of new friends at the "Hottest Show on Earth" in Albuquerque, New Mexico. Or you may wish to journey to the "Hokitika Wild Foods Festival" in New Zealand's South Island to sample "palate-challenging fare, from chocolate-dipped chilies to stallion-semen protein shots!" Note the exclamation mark and tremble.

There are different types of chili for making chocolate, harissa, and chili con carne; chilies for Szechuan chicken and vindaloo; and chilies so potent they are said to make Japanese warriors invincible. There are also sauces so hot they could kill you. Go on, tell us about them! Bore us with a list of the chili's botanical relations, bang on about the pleasure/pain principle and the addictive endorphin high, regale us with recipes for Javanese soups made with boiled chili leaves, and tell us again about that mouth-numbing chili cheese you ate with the monks in Bhutan. But please, please, please don't produce another bottle of Dave's Private Reserve Insanity Sauce. Still haven't made a dent in the one you gave us 10 years ago.

Fig. 20
A chili reception

Chili Bore 53

Coffee—Not As Simple As You Think

Good coffee needs seriously expensive, chrome-plated machinery that hisses, as well as pressure gauges, measuring gadgets, special cups, jugs, spoons, frothers, dampers, teeny tiny spoons, special sugar lumps, things called groups, people called baristas, and, sometimes, just a little twist of lemon. Then come the beans. No simple choice of strong, medium, or weak here; coffee beans are like grapes in their complexity and their reaction to sunshine, rain, and soil. They also come with a plethora of political baggage, so you also have to worry about slave labor in coffee plantations and please check the human-rights record of the country of origin before you buy. Thank you.

And now for the roast and, of course, different beans from different vintages react in different ways in different ovens, so, really, you'll have to buy a nice, glossy coffee table book to find your way around. Don't have a coffee table? Add it to the list. Now for the grind. That depends entirely on how you make your coffee, so that's not simple either. And here's a thing: even if you think, that's okay, I have an espresso machine, it's chrome-plated and it hisses, that's not enough info. The coffee-grinding person in the specialty coffee-bean shop will require the make of your machine, what kind of water you use, the humidity in the air on any given day of the week, and the hour, day, and month of your birth.

So, the question is this: does the real foodie have enough money in the bank, enough time, and sufficient brain space for all this? And I have to say that one of the nicest and sanest foodies I know doesn't "do" coffee at all. Maybe this is the way forward.

Fig. 21
That wrong kind of water

Coffee–Not As Simple As You Think

The Tea Ceremony

The tea buff's world revolves around special, rare, and organic leaves courtesy of furtive, members-only Internet sites. Obviously, no tea bags and no messing about...due ceremony must be given to the process: the precious liquid brewed in beautiful pots and drunk from thin porcelain cups. Aaah! Many happy hours pass agreeably in tea-buff land, cucumber sandwiches curling on the plate, afternoon sun gleaming on the silver sugar tongs, and the sound of sophisticated chatter on the merits of Assam Hazelbank, the delicacy of Chui Fong, and the excitement surrounding the latest release of Mao Jian spring green tea.

There's really no way to trump the tea buff; they're on a predictable path to perfection. So, it's time to wish them well, wave goodbye, and head off in the other direction—back to the tea ceremony that keeps lumberjacks' chainsaws humming and swagmen criss-crossing the outback in search of farm work: billy tea. The foodie has done his research and repaired to the bottom of the garden. First, he builds a fire and constructs a support for the metal rod that will hold the billy can over the flames. Next, he fills the can with water and sits poking at the fire, dreaming about being "home on the range" instead of back in the office on Monday morning. When the first bubbles appear, in goes a manly handful of cheap, dark tea leaves and then, when the water really starts to boil, the contents of a can of condensed milk. Stir with a cleanish stick, wait a moment for the bulk of the leaves to sink to the bottom of the can, and serve immediately in chipped enamel mugs. If second or third helpings are required, simply pour more water on the exhausted leaves and repeat the process of boiling and adding condensed milk.

In the Foodie Kitchen

Fig. 21

Fine china doesn't cut it when you got a bucket

The Ages of Vinegar

Time to take a stand and lead the pack in the opposite direction. What's wrong with ordinary vinegar for goodness' sake? It's traditional, it's local, it's been around for centuries, it's mostly water, and it's so cheap, it's a joke. You can use it to rinse your washing, clean your fish tank, condition your dreadlocks, kill weeds, stop cats in their tracks, and pickle onions. It contains no fat, cholesterol, fiber, or sugar. It can relieve high blood pressure, cure eczema, heal wounds, relieve jellyfish and bee stings, fight dandruff, and remove warts.

But, on the other hand, if someone were to offer to sell you a tiny bottle of *Aceto Balsamico Tradizionale di Reggio Emilia*, aged in mulberry and juniper wood casks for 25 years...what would you say? And they'd probably also tell you that there's little point in buying unaged balsamic because it's not THE REAL THING. Imagine this nectar drizzled onto your strawberries, just staining an exquisite gelato, or served as a precious little puddle to dunk your bread and cheese. Tempted?

Wake up, man! It costs 199.99 a bottle (admittedly as part of a gift set with an overwrought glass jug and a padded box). Get with the distilled malt and act like it's the new thing. Add a bit of sugar, boil it up a bit—it'll get sticky enough to drizzle on something and, as an added bonus, you can dab some on a soft cloth and remove that unsightly glue patch from your car left by that "Garlic Is Not Just For Breakfast" bumper sticker.

Fig. 23

"They'll never believe me back in Modena!"

The Ages of Vinegar

The Chastity
of Olive Oil

The virgins are kept in a cool, dark cupboard under the stairs. This one is infused with mandarin oil, that one with chili. Over there behind the vacuum cleaner is a range of garlic oils: summer garlic, wild garlic from the garden in the south of France, and a bio-dynamic smoked garlic oil which is just out-of-this-world drizzled over sourdough bread. The herb-suffused oils are next to the mop and bucket. That's a sprig of wild tarragon plucked from a south-facing hedgerow in the hills above Saint-Paul-de-Vence on the French Riviera; the next one's basil from a friend's windowsill that overlooks Santa Maria di Novella in Firenze...sorry, Florence. The single-estate oils are all labeled with their provenance...Tuscan ones here, Moroccan there, and so on.

Cook with them! Are you mad? See that one? Ultra-premium oil from Crete! Practically hand-made by Orthodox monks from this little grove of the oldest olive trees in the world! They produce 500 bottles a year, tops! You can't be sploshing that on your salad! Maybe a drizzle as a finishing flourish, or a little puddle in a tiny bowl for friends who can appreciate this kind of thing—and, frankly, not many do. No, for everyday we use this laid-back, sweet, fruity little number from Liguria: low acidity, fresh avocado undertones, and a delicate, peppery finish. An excellent all-rounder. We get it from Supa-Save.

Fig. 24

"Okay Nigel! The mop and bucket are going in your side of the bed."

The Chastity of Olive Oil

The Sun-Dried Tomato

You know you love them! Little bursts of tomatoey-ness personified, brilliant little stabs of flavor in salads and stews, but like every "fashionable" ingredient that is perhaps a bit overused in the initial burst of enthusiasm, the foodie must move on and learn to sneer at his old, industrially-sun-dried friend, plucked from the supermarket shelf in its handy jar of rather ordinary olive oil. He must bite the bullet. He must dry his own tomatoes, risk his neck, and get with the program.

"It's no bother at all, really it isn't. You just cut the tomatoes in half, place them on racks, sprinkle with sea salt, and wait for the weather forecast to predict a good, long sunny spell. Climb up on your roof and lay out the tomatoes (this charming peasant family in Puglia showed us all this when we were down there last summer—even sold us their racks). So, you let the tomatoes give up their moisture to the midday sun, and then climb up again at dusk and carefully bring all the racks back into the house—otherwise, the dew undoes all that good work. Then repeat the process, day by day, by day, by day. In a couple of weeks, there you have it. And you only need about 100 tomatoes to get a jar full. And we've got the racks, so no excuses there. And, like I said, no bother at all."

Fig. 25

"*He's trying his best to please us, but frankly, I prefer the stale bread in the park*"

The Sun-Dried Tomato

Salt

And you thought you were on safe ground here? Well, scientists will tell you (and so will Wikipedia) that salt is basically sodium and chloride ions which are essential in small quantities for all known living creatures to regulate the water content of their bodies. And that is why we have table salt—a vital culinary condiment that pours so easily from little drums or cardboard packs, is gratifyingly cheap, and helpfully laced with iodine (also vital for life).

But the foodie has quite different ideas on how to regulate the water content of his body. Have a peek in his salt cupboard. Pink Himalayan crystal salt (if you believe the label) is 250 million years old and as pure as the ancient primal oceans. Let's just hope it isn't mined from chunks of Himalaya that are home to decomposing climbers and a million discarded ready-meals. Hawaiian black lava salt with charcoal? On your fries? No thanks. Blue salt from a salt mine in Iran! Head swimming with images of salt miners lashed into submission by frenzied Mullahs and salt rubbed into wounds. Can't go there, sorry! Unappetizingly gray sea salt flakes inconveniently packed into a little designer canvas bag...nothing wrong with the sea is there? Fish don't piss in it or anything, do they? Am longing for that damp little screw of blue paper that they used to put in bags of potato chips. You knew where that came from: a proper, clean, and tidy salt factory run by happy workers in hairnets who had clean fingernails.

Fig. 26

An intrepid foodie proving he's worth his salt

The Truffle Shaver

The utensil drawers have been specially made because no manufacturer of kitchen units can have possibly foreseen either the amount or the bulky nature of the foodies' vital kitchen equipment. In the grating and shaving section, he has an assortment of micro-planes—about half a dozen at the last count, all with different gauges of rasp for grating cheese, zesting lemons, and shredding things (but not truffles). And it's amazing the damage you can do to your knuckles rummaging about in that little collection. There is also a heavy-duty mandoline for turning vegetables into a pile of shaven strips. The truffle shaver, where all this began, is different yet again because it has an adjustable blade depending on how generous you wish to be; it is quite a handsome device to use at the table, and it is obviously impossible to shave a truffle with anything else.

Forks for prodding, tongs for turning, thermometers for meat and sugar, and measuring spoons and cups—he's got all of those. Potato mashers are for crushing things, a potato ricer is actually for mashing potatoes, and a potato peeler is for shaving Parmesan cheese. The melon baller? It's for taking seeds out of tomatoes. If you've got all day, we could visit his electrical appliances cupboard with a lot of shiny chrome machines for mixing and blending, churning ice cream, and stuffing sausages.

Next week he'll probably put all this stuff on eBay and "go commando" with a knife and a wooden spoon. Probably not just the one knife, though, as it would not be too far from the truth to say that he is in love with his knives—and the knife drawer has slots for each of his best beloveds. He will throw a fit if anyone else picks one up and a spectacular tantrum if it is put away in the wrong slot. Suffice to say, his knife collection has been beefed up with some pretty vicious blades from Japan, so, on the whole, it's best to leave his knives alone.

Fig. 27
"You're mine, all mine!"

Wine Gift Overload

You wish to buy a caring gift that recognizes your foodie friend's main interest in life without straying too far into his territory or betraying your own lack of interest or expertise. Kitchen utensils are out, as no one buys a professional the tools of his trade. He will very likely consider the most recherché of ingredients you can find *ordinaire* beyond belief, while playful, amusing aprons may offend as they suggest food preparation is a light-hearted pursuit and he probably kits himself out in chef's whites to make toast. Dish cloths are the foodie equivalent of socks. An esoteric, wine-related present, however, is a safe gift and that is why the serious wino/foodie will have accumulated a cupboard full of novelty corkscrews, wine thermometers, silver bottle labels, amusing bottle stoppers, designer bottle stoppers, wine-bottle coasters, curious caddies and cradles for red wine with winding mechanisms for the perfect pour, and a dazzling assortment of coolers and chillers.

His nearest and dearest will have ripped open their wallets to buy him hardcore wine-bottle-opening kits presented in fuzzy, velvet-lined boxes with foil cutters and serious lever-action devices with 31 moving parts. He will have a cupboard full of decanters, both ancient and modern, with curious breathing holes and swirling chambers, as well as glorious crystal glasses for every kind of wine in sets of two, with no one set matching another.

So, next time you are wondering: "What can we for buy the foodie?", give him a break, put down that wine-tasting diary, and buy the man a pair of slippers.

Fig. 28
Dear Santa, next year: 1) A whole leg of Iberico ham,
2) Tartan slippers, 3) An early start to Lent

Wine Gift Overload

CHAPTER 3
The Foodie Out and About

Adventures with Wine

There is a chapter in Hugh Johnson's seminal work—*Wine: A Life Uncorked*—entitled "The Wilder Shores of Wine." The foodie's eyes lit up as he downed this chapter in one (along with the realization that exploring mainstream wine leaves you trailing in the wake of Masters). Like picking a subject for the TV show Mastermind, the foodie decided to drill deep in a very small area and swot up on the wines of Africa. Specifically, the more challenging areas of the continent where there are few wines with any reputation, but a lot of interesting tussles with the *terroir*, plenty of fascinating tales of grapes triumphing over climate, and inventive kick-starts to the wine-making process such as opium or a couple of aspirin (don't try this at home).

On holiday in exotic Kasbah country, the foodie impresses fellow travellers with his enthusiasm for the local wines. Taste! Smell! Absorb the enigmatic, elusive flavors, the pungent nose, and earthy undertones that make this wine a perfect partner for the spicy, ricey indigenous peasant cuisine! Pausing only to drink deep, he shifts into poetic overdrive as he describes the vines' persistent roots fighting the adverse conditions of the sun-baked land to deliver into their glasses the very essence of this place— the distillation of the earth beneath their feet. And, as he gushes on (and on), some members of the party actually look around at this fabled earth beneath their feet, which has been distilled so poignantly and poetically into their slightly greasy glasses and start to feel queasy. Pigeons flap and squabble around their table. Feral cats yowl and fight around open garbage cans. A dog shits lavishly. An old man hawks and spits. The enigmatic, elusive flavors and earthy undertones suddenly zing into focus.

Beers all round, I think.

Fig. 29

*"A humble young wine without antecedents,
but I think you'll be bemused by its assumptions"*

The Language of Wine

There are only so many times the foodie can listen to ever-livelier versions of his North African wine disaster (see page 72), which neatly explains his presence on a Wine Appreciation Course run by a noted Master of Wine. Assembled in a polished, paneled, and perfectly proportioned tasting room, the foodie and his fellow students are welcomed by the Master, enthused by his passionate exhortation to taste sympathetically, to apply all their senses to the wine, to observe it, nose it, and taste it. The Master's bravura performance, his expert swirl of the glass, his acute eye for hue, his assured sniff, his practised, lip-smacking gargle and spit—all these impress the foodie no end, but not nearly as much as the language! Yellow amber gold, deep garnet ruby, woody, beefy, nutty, flabby, dumb, thin, fat, gritty, the taste of old straw, bitter walnuts...the challenge is to describe a nuance of color, a fleeting aroma, to conjure a taste with words. "Be inventive!" urges the Master. "Be instinctive!" "This," thinks the foodie, "I can do."

And he did excel himself. He would draw on every smell he'd ever smelt, every taste he'd ever registered, all his life's experiences. He would out-language the lot of them. Wine is poured, glasses swirled, color observed, aromas inhaled, and words like "dry," "thin," "tannin," and "brittle" are bandied about to the Master's nodding approval. The foodie thinks for a moment and then a memory pops into his mind.

"Um...new shoes...yes, no, wait a minute, the box, that's it! The cardboard box that had my wife's high heels in it, about an hour or so after she'd taken them out."

The room falls silent.

"Interesting," pronounces the Master. "And this one?"

The foodie's on a roll. "Warm, powdery, dusty, rosy...maybe a hamster cage, no, hold on...it's my Gran's dressing table...her face powder..."

Fellow students have instinctively given the foodie some space. The Master hands him another glass and retreats toward the door. The foodie swirls and sniffs with a confident swagger. He's getting the hang of it now! "Freshly dead budgerigar in a field of daffodils...on a warm Sunday afternoon in July!"

*Fig.*30
Chateau Talbot 2009

_____

"You could take the view," said the Master of Wine to colleagues later that day over a pie and pint in the Cork & Bottle, "that we have unearthed a deeply troubled transvestite pet-killer. More charitably, there is the possibility that we have found an "interesting" new voice in the world of wine. Either way, my advice is to steer well clear."

Market Day

It is his tiresome over-confidence that usually leads to the difficulties...over-confidence coupled with a determination to be different which have him believe that wherever he goes on holiday, food producers and market traders simply cannot wait to interact with a true foodie—language no barrier. He is determinedly not a tourist; he will not be buying tomatoes, mushrooms, or lettuce. Chicken is for wimps. He will listen, he will learn, he will embrace the food that is truly theirs. He will make their day, become their new best friend, and be taken unto their bosom. They will teach him how to braise cow's udders and attempt to marry him off to their daughters. Who needs a dictionary? Food is a universal language absorbed through tastes, smells, gestures, and understanding.

He bounces into action on market day, festooned with ethnic baskets to blend in with the locals as he shops. He will return, baskets laden with indigenous produce and local know-how, to rustle up a memorable feast that he looks forward to re-living many, many times in years to come—a regional dish so complex that it is only ever eaten once a year by the men of the household on St. Whatsit's Day. (Given what we now know, he got that bit of information very wrong. It wasn't a recipe at all—it was directions to the public latrines.)

But he had a wonderful time at the market! He bought dirty little cheeses smelling of goat's droppings from a simple young man with a disturbing smile who will be coming to stay for a week or two in September. He has a fistful of limp bitter leaves, bought from a bent-double widow with rheumy eyes and no teeth, and the long skinny tail of an animal that he couldn't quite get the name of, but which he was forced to buy from her cousin at knife-point. So colorful, these people! The foodie is interacting like mad! He has knobbly vegetables, bread that is dark and dangerous, small grubby things that wiggle, and lumps of brownish spongy stuff that again he couldn't quite get the name of, but was assured was vital to his dish.

The market haul, laid out in the ill-equipped holiday kitchen, looks unpromising. Not a single item you could point to and recognize apart from the tail of something. His friends, for whom memories are still vivid of the "Unfortunate Incident" in Crete with the goat foetus and the "Misunderstanding in Omsk" over the beaver tail, have wisely booked a table at a local taverna. Will he ever learn?

Fig. 31
Bartering with the locals

Three-Star Dining

The foodie and his friends, Peregrine Posh and Jonny Dash are treating themselves to a fine-dining experience in a hallowed cathedral of *haute cuisine*. Wives/partners will not be joining them—this is a foodie outing. Besides, Peregrine's wife has run off with the gardener, and he needs cheering up.

The friends enter the sanctuary—the holy of holies. There are few regular diners in a place like this; most are parties of foodies who have travelled from Wakayama, Wolverhampton, and Wyoming expecting nothing less than nirvana on a plate. Voices are hushed in reverence. Ushered to their table, they pass a pair of Japanese foodies, taking notes and snapping every artful smear of purée from every angle. The Maître D gives just a hint of a disapproving sniff and Nigel resolves to leave his notebook in his pocket. Seated at the altar, sorry the table, they hardly have time to admire the silver and sparkle of their surroundings and the starched, craftily folded napkins before they are engulfed in a warm blanket of solicitous service and amusing, whimsical mouthfuls with the compliments of the chef.

Peregrine chooses a moment to embark on his woeful tale of marital troubles just as a waiting person arrives to whisk away a breadcrumb. Spell broken, talk turns to the food: "*Sous vide*, definitely *sous vide*!" "What's the elusive flavor in that foam?" "Such an inspired touch, that licorice!" All is rich and rare, each plate a work of art. But Peregrine's chin wobbles. There is so much he needs to say. A tear involuntarily trickles down a cheek, the others look up from their very large plates with very small blobs of food, concerned for their dear friend, but a waiter appears from nowhere to proffer Peregrine a tissue and, once again, the moment passes and their attention is diverted by the sausage and potato ice cream. Peregrine seizes another opportunity to unburden his soul just as the Maître D glides over to ask if their chosen dishes have lived up to expectations and they are off again, trying to identify the crunchy bits in the pumpkin dariole.

Such is the power of the three-star restaurant—outside troubles dare not intrude.

Fig.32
"We are trained to feel your pain, sir"

Lovingly Hand-Written in *Jus*

You can see how it started. A restaurateur puts filet mignon and sautéed potatoes on his menu followed by a hefty price tag. But it doesn't tell the whole story. It doesn't even begin to explain the effort that has gone into this simple dish.

His beef comes from this little farm in a valley with the juiciest grass. The cattle all have names (not just numbers), and the farmer goes out to check his cattle every evening, pats them on the head, and chats to them about life and the universe and everything. When the time comes, they get chauffeur-driven to slaughter in a really nice truck with soothing classical music on the stereo. The potatoes are cultivated from a rare heritage seed crop in bio-dynamic soil. Planted when the moon waxes, dug up by hand when the moon wanes, and rushed to the restaurant before sunrise with the wholesome earth still clinging to them. They are hand-washed in spring water, cut infuriatingly slowly into wedges by his elderly mother-in-law with her favorite Opinel knife, and dabbed dry with linen dish towels. And, if he replaced her with someone younger and quicker, it would be divorce and he'd lose the restaurant. Explain that to the punters!

Steak et frites   22.50

Filet mignon from the well-hung carcass of Alphonse, lovingly raised by his natural mother, treated to an organic diet of hand-selected tender grass, exercised daily by an Australian personal trainer to ensure layers of muscle growth and marbled fat. He met his end to the relaxing strains of the adagio movement of Bach's Opus 110. Our chef has seared this cut to perfection (see page 94 of this menu for a full and fascinating description of the pepper sauce). It comes to your plate nestled enticingly alongside our exclusive sautéed potatoes— hand-picked by moonlight, carefully washed, painstakingly hand-cut, and hand-dabbed dry with absolutely no concept of hurry by an interfering old pensioner who refuses to concede her place in the kitchen or her iron grip on the gin bottle. They are then triple-cooked in beef dripping and seasoned with rosemary-infused sea salt.

Too much information!

Fig.33
A potato is a potato is a potato, except in this establishment, obviously

Your Usual Table

It's a pleasure to be recognized at your neighborhood restaurant. Nice to feel your custom is appreciated and, especially for the foodie, to feel surrounded by professionals who value his many opinions and helpful suggestions. He likes to take friends to *La Solita Tavola* to impress them with how well known he is to all the staff: "Hello Nigel! How's the family? Bunions still giving you grief?" He likes his friends to know that in the world of restaurants, he is a first among equals and the management accept him as a fellow foodie who knows his stuff. "We have some wonderful chanterelles in today, Nigel! How about we make you a risotto, just for you! Just the way you like it!"

The foodie is the first to concede (sometimes a little too loudly) that this is by no means a first-class establishment, but what they do, they do okay, as well as to infer that the establishment would have to close without his input. He's the guy who suggested they put cream in their *Pasta Alla Primavera*, who persuaded them to change olive supplier, and gave them a recipe for spinach gnocchi he got from somebody's granny in Tuscany. Not that they serve it that often.

A quick peek behind the scenes reveals just what pros these guys are.

"Oh gawd. It's Know-it-All Nigel at table six, with a bunch of his pretentious pals," groans the Maître D, banging his head on a tray. "That's twice in one week!"

"*Il stupido* who desecrate my primavera with cream?"

"Yeah him."

"Tries to tell me, Guiseppe Barolo, how to make gnocchi when I learn at my mamma's knee?"

"That would be Nigel!"

"I spit in 'is food!"

"I know you do, chef. I tread on his bunions."

Fig. 34

"Tell chef I'll let him have my sister's recipe for caponata"

I'll Order for You, Shall I?

INT. RESTAURANT. EVENING.
This is an up-market establishment: white nappery
dazzles, soft lights gleam, patient waiters hover.
Three friends, NIGEL, PEREGRINE, and JONNY, are
seated at a corner table, studying their menus.

JONNY

All looks a bit much, really...

PEREGRINE

Quite fancy the guinea fowl.
Nanny used to make these scrummy pies...

NIGEL

You don't come to a place like this to
eat chicken pie! Look, there's a risotto
with sea-urchin and pumpkin...

JONNY

Soup, I could go for the roast tomato soup without
the fancy-dan bits...

NIGEL

I really think you should try the brioche stuffed
with crab and samphire foam...

JONNY

No mate, soup. Definitely soup. And the duck.

Peregrine puts his menu down, decisively, on the table.

PEREGRINE

Pâté with pickles. Sounds good to me. Then the pie.

A WAITER appears, as if by magic, pen hovering over
his order pad.

WAITER

So, have you made your selection, gentlemen?

PEREGRINE

Yes! I'll have the p...

NIGEL

No, look, Perry. You can't come here and eat pâté...
like you can't order tomato soup...

PEREGRINE

Why not? I like pâté.

JONNY

You're such a wanker, Nigel.

WAITER

(startled to hear such language
in a hallowed temple of food)
I'll...I'll just give you...gentlemen...
a few moments...

...And the waiter melts away.

PEREGRINE

What have you got against pâté?

                              NIGEL

        Nothing! But it's not a true test of the kitchen!

                            PEREGRINE

       In my world, Nigel, the purpose of a kitchen is to
                  make you something you want to eat.

                              JONNY

                      Like soup and duck.

                              NIGEL

                    (reading from the menu)
        Pacific Ocean black cod filet on a creamy pearl
                    barley risotto infused...

                              JONNY

                Waiter! We're ready to order...

        The waiter glides into view.

                              JONNY

             (cont'd, sotto voce to the waiter)
        Sorry about the wanker thing back there, but can you
             see what we're dealing with here? I'll have the
                      soup...and the duck.

                              WAITER

                       Very good, sir.

                              NIGEL

                   (sounding a little shrill)
        NO, no. He's not going to have soup! We'll have the
        sea urchin risotto, the brioche, and the carpaccio of
            swordfish; that way, we can all have a taste...

                            JONNY

   Swordfish are humming with mercury, mate—you don't
   want to be eating that. I certainly don't want to be
                       eating that...

                            NIGEL

   For the main course, I'll have the cod, he'll have the
   braised ox-cheek wrapped in a duxelle of...whatever,
   and forget the duck. He's having the lobster raviolo
             drizzled with pomegranate jus and...

                           WAITER

   Excellent choice, gentlemen. The sommelier will be
                      with you shortly.

   He tucks away his notebook and glides to the kitchen.

                          PEREGRINE

   Choice! We're eating with The Foodie. What choice do
                         we have!

                            NIGEL

       Look guys, if you don't increase your knowledge,
    challenge your tastebuds, you're nowhere. Soup, pies,
   pâté, for Christ's sake! Pomegranate and lobster! That
   could be inspired! Crab and aniseed. I mean this could
   be ground-breaking stuff...I'm really looking forward
        to your girolles and chorizo mousse, Jonny.

                            JONNY

             Afterwards, I'm having the cheeseboard.
               All. To. My. Self. Understood?

   FADE TO BLACK...

Nigel@foodieblog.com

My wife Jane has gone to stay with her mother, taking our daughter with her, and I am not quite sure how long they will be gone this time. It may have had something to do with my attempts to barbecue a whole hog in the back yard. Her rose bed, as she pointed out quite forcefully before running up the stairs to pack her bags, does look like a scene from *Apocalypse Now*.

Some weeks earlier I had booked a reconciliatory treat for Jane (and her mother) at *La Table Bien Preparé*. This was in recognition of her patience over the exploding espresso machine incident that I blogged about last month. However, bookings at *La Table* being so hard to come by, I was not about to pass up on the treat and I invited along two of my best friends, Peregrine (who was raised by nannies in a stately home) and Jonny (who is Australian). I share this only so that you know where their palates come from.

First impressions: La Table Bien Preparé, which means the well-laid table in English, has a lovely *ambience* and, obviously, they do care a great deal about the way the tables are laid. Jonny complained about the number of knives and forks and fancy, useless plates, but Peregrine flicked out his napkin as to the manor born.
8/10

The complimentary amuse-bouche: The liver foam was too salty and the pastry on the kidney profiteroles was soggy. Jonny refused to touch any of these. Peregrine waved his spoon about, but I noticed he didn't eat any. I think "variety meats" in pastry is maybe a concept too far for an appetizer.

2/10

RISOTTO, PHOTOGRAPHED UNDER EXTREME DURESS

The first courses: We decided that in order to get the best from this gastronomic experience, we would share a trio of appetizers. Normally, on my restaurant blogs, as loyal followers will know, I take photographs of every dish, but my companions had threatened to castrate me if I did so on this occasion. The sea urchin and pumpkin risotto was well made, but could have done with some punchier flavors. A brioche stuffed with crab was the winner, but Jonny let loose with some choice Australian expressions to describe the samphire foam. I found the carpaccio of swordfish faultless.

5/10

The main courses: Lobster, parsnip, and pomegranate are a bold combination; sometimes these things work and sometimes they don't. I will not be trying this at home. The black cod was beautifully cooked, but Jonny made a huge a fuss about the accompanying risotto until the chef grudgingly came up with a serving of French fries. I nearly died of shame. The ox-cheek Wellington with girolle and chorizo mousse was perhaps the best dish of the night, in my opinion, as the others wouldn't touch it. More fool them. It was meltingly rich and full of textured surprises.

4/10

Dessert: The evening deteriorated from this moment on. Jonny ate his own body weight in cheese and Peregrine forced the chef to make him apple pie and custard even though it wasn't on the menu. My organic blackcurrant soufflé with apple and sorrel sorbet was divine.

3/10

Overall: 4/10 Nigelpoints

Personally, I rated the cooking skills and inventiveness high (if sometimes misguided), but my companions did not rate the experience at all, giving everything 0 out of 10 (except for the cheeseboard which Jonny rated as a 10+). And, according to the rules of my blog, their views have to be taken into consideration. Peregrine was only consoled by the pie, while Jonny said something very offensive to the waiter about the ratio of expertize on the table-laying/cooking axis. He may have been suffering from cheese-rage.

The Pop Up

What does the foodie really want? In an ideal world, he would give up his middle management job at the Passport Office to (a) become a restaurant critic on a national newspaper or a glossy magazine or (b) open a successful restaurant.

He blogs away in the hope of being discovered as a critic but has a way to go, as I am sure you will agree (see page 88). Option (b) is a tough call. I am sure very few people set out to open restaurants that are both culinary and financial disasters, but it is amazing how many do. The foodie, however, has a wise and cautious wife who is good at logistics and creating spreadsheets. They have decided to put a toe in the water (this is management-speak in case you think we are all going to the seaside in the next sentence) with a pop-up restaurant in a friend's double-car garage. It is to operate only on Saturday nights by subscription; it is to be called *The Deconstructed Fishcake* because basically that's all there is on the menu. To register for an opportunity to visit, email nigel@foodieblog.com, it would cheer him up no end.

The fishcakes are the foodie's signature dish and they are exceptionally good; he's been perfecting the recipe for years. He miraculously makes his fishcakes out of flaked fish, and only flaked fish and flavorings—well, alright, a tiny bit of mayo, a light coating of crumb—and they somehow hold together. And he serves all kinds of flavorful creamy mashed potato on the side: olive-oil mash, celeriac mash—

you choose. There's a good choice of fishcakes too—the black cod with capers, parsley, lemon zest, and anchovies is my favorite. But what a great idea for a pop-up! Or so it seemed at the time. What could go wrong? All he has to do is make tons of fishcakes, mash up a million potatoes, stay calm, and pan fry to order.

He was actually dreaming of opening *Deconstructed Fishcake Parlors* in every major city, appearing on TV with Gordon Ramsay, signing copies of *The Deconstructed Fishcake Cookbook*, but, sad to say, it's never going to happen. The first Saturday just about went okay because he'd taken a week off work to prepare and all his friends rallied round on the promise of free fishcakes.

Sadly, his dreams of a global fishcake empire stalled on week two in a slurry of overcooked mash, crumbling fishcakes, a sobbing wife, an exploding chemical toilet, an unhappy health-and-safety officer, a wine delivery that never made it through, and several hyperventilating punters with bones stuck in their throats. Making fishcakes the foodie way is not something he can delegate or hurry. Feeding paying customers is not a job for the amateur, as Gordon Ramsay would no doubt have told him in a colorful kind of way. Dream on hold.

Fig.35
What could possibly go wrong?

The Pop Up

Adventurous Eating to No Purpose

Some handy hints for the foodie who wishes to experiment with "exotic" meats. This is what they taste like (allegedly)...

Alligator   Cross between a rubbery chicken and a tough rabbit

Bear   A bit like very dense beef. Bear fat is rank. Cook well as the meat contains parasites.

Beaver tail   An acquired taste. If you don't have to eat it, I wouldn't if I were you.

Cat   People guess it tastes like very unpleasant chicken with a parasite problem, but it is hard to find anyone (even on the Internet) who will own up to cooking kitty.

Crocodile   Bland, salty chicken

Dog   Stringy beef. In Korea (apparently), you may choose to have it bitter-tasting with adrenalin (when the dog has been beaten up prior to death) or sweeter-tasting (when it has been humanely killed). This is food for drunk men.

Hamsters   Bitter and very tough chicken

Hedgehogs	*See* **Hamsters**
Insects	Crunchy if they have exoskeletons; prawn texture inside but no taste
Kangaroo	Like venison, but tougher
Ostrich	Veal or mild beef. If overcooked, it tastes like liver. But there are many fans of this low-cholesterol meat.
Possum	Fishy, tough, crocodiley chicken
Rattlesnake	Very badly cooked, dry chicken
Squirrel	Gamey chicken. Younger squirrels have more tender meat
Turtle	Frog's legs, which in turn taste remarkably similar to chicken
Whale	Musky, dense, unpleasant, and extremely tough beef. The only surprise is that it doesn't taste remotely of fish.

The moral of the story: in most cases, stick to chicken.

On the Ethnic Trail

The foodie takes his curiosity out to eat a lot. "Chinese" or "Indian" or "Japanese'"are categories too broad for him. He wants to track down the specialists in Burmese salted fish and the sweet, sour, salty dishes of Cambodia. On speed dial for Indian take-outs he has a Goan restaurant because he is conducting research into their fishcakes, and a Maharashtrian hole-in-the-wall type of establishment where he tasted an intricate dish of garlicky, gingery vegetables that he's still trying to recreate.

But he has learnt to his cost (as we all have) that just because a person who opens a restaurant is from Goa, for example, it does not naturally follow that that person is a cook of any distinction. He had a nasty experience in a Czech restaurant involving grease and dumplings, and an equally unpleasant, sour-cabbage-soup moment in a Romanian establishment. Not to be daunted, he's scooped up unidentifiable stew with his fingers in a small Ethiopian café where everyone laughed at him when he asked for a fork.

To be fair, his quest has delivered good experiences along with the bad. Good in that he has been able to dine out on the story of tracking down an elusive Bolivian dish called Pique Macho only to discover it was an unappetizing heap of chopped beef, chopped hot dog, fries, boiled eggs, mayonnaise, and ketchup. Very reminiscent of the food he ate as a student, and he honestly thought that he would never be faced with the like again. How the indigenous Inca population of Bolivia got their hands on ketchup, mayonnaise, and hot dogs is puzzling him still.

Fig. 36

An authentic Amazonian welcoming feast

CHAPTER 4
The Foodie
Lifestyle

What Foodies Read

Never mind the plots, Enid Blyton could write a good picnic. Spread out before the Famous Five were tomato sandwiches, ginger beer, lemonade, cans of sardines, lettuces, radishes, and, tellingly, lashings of boiled eggs and a screw of salt. It's the salt that does it. An egg without salt is rubbish, and that little thought would have lodged in the mind of our fledgling foodie, long after the thrilling scene where Timmy the dog savaged the evil foreign baddies was forgotten. (Or was George the dog?)

Milly Molly Mandy—now, there was a girl who knew the importance of a reliable supplier—ready with her toasting fork in front of the fire waiting for the Saturday delivery by the muffin man, strawberry jam and cherry cake to hand. An impeccable role model, unlike Just William, whose diet of pear drops, licorice sticks, boiled sweets, and squashed toffees extracted from sticky pockets is enough to make any young foodie shudder with disgust.

Growing up, our foodie would have found much delight in Charles Dickens' gargantuan feast of novels, replete with pigeon pies, roasted hams, and oysters. He may also have re-read *Moby Dick* several times just to check the recipe for clam chowder "enriched with butter, and plentifully seasoned with pepper and salt."

Novels that are almost cookbooks are a dead give-away for spotting the off-duty foodie relaxing on the beach between market trips, truffle hunts, and private wine-tastings. There are many to choose from, and everyone will have opinions and favorites in this category, but outstanding contenders have to be any one of Patricia's Cornwell's Kay Scarpetta books (you could practically cook a meal off the page) and, as for Donna Leon's Inspector Brunetti, the mystery is how he makes time for solving any crimes at all when there's so much mouth-watering lunching going on at his dining table.

Fig. 37
"I'm only reading this for the mouth-watering description of bouillabaisse on page 94"

Foodie Myths

It's difficult to know where to start here... so many apocryphal tales: like chewing gum taking seven years to digest, which is wrong and eating fish making you smarter, which could actually be true. Here are a few more:

Myth: You can eat magnificently anywhere in France for a fiver.
Reality: Bollocks. You can eat restaurant food as boring and horrible in France as you can anywhere else. Being French does not mean you can cook. In fact, many French people rely utterly on their neighborhood *traiteur* to cook their supper.

Myth: Organic produce is better for you and better for the planet.
Reality: Not necessarily. Conventional farming methods put nutrients back into the soil, use pesticides that work effectively, and seeds resistant to pests so that less pesticide needs to be used. Organic food is less efficiently farmed and, while its pesticides may be "natural," some can be more hazardous to human health and the water table than scientifically developed ones. In the end, organic produce is about taste and not saving the planet. Sorry, foodie.

Myth: Oysters are an aphrodisiac.
Reality: Not if you have ever eaten a bad one. A bad-oyster vomiting fit is the least sexy thing on earth. I know this to be true.

Myth: Eating an ortolan is THE top foodie experience of all time.
Reality: If you like that sort of thing. The poor little bird is captured alive, kept in the dark, force fed oats to make it swell up, drowned in brandy, and then roasted. Diners crunch the carcass all in one mouthful and drape a napkin over their heads,

supposedly to keep the aromas concentrated. More likely this is to hide their sin from the gods and their identity from the police, as eating ortolan is illegal.

Myth: German scientists put the decimal point in the wrong place when calculating the iron content of spinach, leading to generations of children being forced to eat spinach and grow up to hate it.
Reality: While the consequence was unfortunately true, it wasn't sloppy fact-checking but bad science that had the world believing spinach was packed with iron. It appears the vessel in which the spinach was heated and the charcoal used to heat it were both to blame for the false reading. But this was back in 1871, so give them a break.

Fig. 38
"Oh Lord, forgive me!"

Foodie Baby Names

Celebs whose relationship with food amounts to ingesting only macrobiotic air and sushi have strayed into this area: Apple and Peaches sound wholesome and sweet, and I'm sure they're very nice little girls who will grow up appreciating their parents' efforts to be different. Come on, foodies. Reclaim your birthright! Take a step beyond the safely fruity and fragrantly herby. Leave Basil, Coriander, and Apricot to the wimps. Here are some hard-core, character-building names to yell across the park. But all names carry baggage:

A

Absinthe (bad reputation as a drink, but sounds melodious)
Aïoli (tragic character in an opera, the one nobody wants to kiss)
Amaretto (let rip with those lovely Italian vowels)
Angostura (best with a McSomething surname; Angostura McDuff will go far in any field of endeavor)
Artichoke (she'll write a best-seller; might be a misery memoir)
Aspic (age will not wither her...)
Aubergine (so much nicer than eggplant)

B

Ballotine (shame this is a bird that's been boned, stuffed, rolled, and tied up with string because it sounds delightful)
Bergamot (a conscientious little swot)
Béarnaise and Béchamel (a nice matching pair of saucy sibling names)
Biscotte (love her already; born to succeed)
Bisque (sister to **Biscotte** and just as delightful)
Borscht (hunts with **Kirsch**)
Bruschetta (a wild child, I think; perpetually a slice of bread short of a sandwich)
Burdock (ideal for a solid kind of child who will study law or accountancy, and be no bother to his parents)

C

Calamari (tender and loving as a baby, will toughen up as he grows)
Canapé (a bit trailer trash, frankly)
Caponata (*see* **Polenta**)
Caramel (one to watch—surprisingly soft under her brittle exterior)
Carbonara (*see* **Polenta**)
Carrot (probably not the nation's number one name choice, but it's snappy...)
Celery (you either love it or hate it)
Chantilly (*see* **Canapé**)
Chard (brave and plucky; a polar explorer's name if ever there was one)
Chickpea (*see* **Peanut**)
Chutney (pleasant, helpful, and sweet, but a little mixed up)
Colcannon (make sure he's of sturdy build, red-haired, and Irish)
Compôte (*see* **Canapé**)
Courgette (*see* **Canapé**)
Croquette (*see* **Canapé**)
Cutlet (this may not go down very well in the playground)

D

Daiquiri (sounds good with a Welsh accent)
Dariole (he's going to work the cruise ships, sorry)

Daube (a papal dynasty beckons. Pope Daube I holding the strings at the Vatican sounds perfectly plausible)

E

Escalope (character in a French movie constantly referred to: *"Ah ce maudit Escalope!"* but never seen)

F

Fennel (*see* **Lettuce and Licorice**)
Fricassé (*see* **Canapé**)

G

Galantine (a dashing gambler/con man)
Garlic (he will be a poet who dabbles in street theater)
Gazpacho (a quiz show host, but a cerebral one)
Gelatin (sister to **Ballotine**)
Gherkin (maybe a career in architecture beckons)
* **Giblet** (Dickensian lawyer—*see* **Gizzard**)
Gizzard (he could only be a stand-up comedy chicken. Along with his unlikely companion **Giblet**, is due to star in the next blockbuster silent movie)

H

Haddock, Haggis, and Hake (an inspired choice for a set of Scottish triplets)
Ham (biblical but tasty)
Hummus (Greek weightlifter)
Hyssop (*see* **Garlic**)

J

Jambalaya (will grow up to be a party person)
Jujube (destined for a career as an unbearably bouncy personal trainer)

K

Kedgeree (mixed-race morning person)
Ketchup (maybe, if you already have a large number of sons whose names all begin with the letter K, this could be your 57th option)
Kirsch (a lock-up-your-daughters type of ski instructor with mirrored sunglasses and rather too snug-fitting lycra. Beware also of **Borscht**)
Kohlrabi (sounds exciting and exotic, but in the end the boy will prove to be disappointingly dull)

Kugelhopf (not a good choice if baby is overweight)
Kumquat (for a fruity name, this one is kick-ass)

L

Lettuce and Licorice (both proper jolly-hockey-sticks names for no-nonsense girls)
Limpet (*see* **Gazpacho**)
Lunch (why not?)

M

Macaroon (another one for the Scots)
Mackerel (and another)
Marinade (bound to bring out the best in her companions)
Meringue (destined to take the dance floor by storm)
Minestrone (minute cellist)
Mollusc (*see* **Cutlet**)
Moussaka (will live in a rose-garlanded cottage in the country, raise 10 children, and become an artist's muse)

N

Noisette, Noodle, Nougat, and Nutmeg (a girl band line-up: the pretty one, the crazy one, the cute fat one, and the one who can sing)

P

Panettone (so much classier than the pedestrian "Tony")
Paprika (eastern European ice dancer)
Pastry (needs some alliteration to really work—team with a middle name like Puff...and watch him grow up to hate you)
Peanut (aahhh! Cute!)
Persimmon (sounds classical and grand; teach the boy Latin and send him to Eton)
Pinot (difficult to cultivate, but complex and rewarding to know)
Pistachio and Prosciutto (will go far in the world of opera)
Polenta (great possibilities here for a celeb of some kind with just the one name...like Madonna)
Pomegranate (*see* **Persimmon**)

Fig. 39
Borscht and Kirsch ready to "instruct" the ladies

Q

Quiche and Quince (nearly Keith and nearly Vince, but not near enough; they will probably have to take up cage fighting)

R

Radicchio (*see* **Prosciutto and Pistachio**—and we have three tenors!)
* **Radish** (edgy politico, very left wing)
Ratatouille (depends on how you say it, but it could be a bit **Canapé**)
Rhubarb (*see* **Cutlet**)
Rissole (solid, dependable, and covered in breadcrumbs)

S

Salsify (a fey kind of girl; probably best friends with **Bruschetta**)
Samphire (new wave British actress)
Scallop (could be into rowing)
Sorbet (*see* **Canapé**)
Soufflé (*see* **Canapé**)
Spinach (avant-garde artist)
Syllabub (Cilla's baby)

T

* **Tapenade** (a tap dancer who will partner **Paprika** to Olympic glory)
Tapioca (fearsomely clever girl, double first, will head up the IMF)
Taramasalata (an opera Diva channelling Maria Callas)
Tomato (*see* **Samphire** or **Spinach**)
Turmeric (*see* **Radish**)

V

Vanilla (*see* **Samphire**)
Vichyssoise (deliciously pretentious; she'll probably marry into royalty)
Vinaigrette (French chanteuse regretting *rien*)

W

Wok and Yam (probably a double act on the comedy circuit)

Z

Zabaglioni (the fourth tenor!)

* Author's top picks

Cheesy Baby Names

What better way for the cheese-lover to celebrate the brilliant diversity of a much-loved dairy food and sandwich filling than to bestow upon a child a name rich in poetry, evocative of place, and redolent with taste memory?

Brie   (on the cheeseboard of life, everybody's second choice)

Camembert   (if he sticks with this and resists the "Bert" temptation, I will be very surprised)

Chabichou   (pert and cheeky; loves to be the center of attention; could potentially grow up to be distinctly creepy)

Chaource   (destined to be a meltingly romantic novelist)

Cheddar   (reliable, down-to-earth country boy)

Dolcelatte   (perfect for a pretty child with a twisted personality)

Edam   (may get confused with Adam)

Epoisse   (dazzling diplomat with a natural ability for sword play)

Feta   (prone to crumbling under pressure)

Fontina   (could pass in the real world; *see* **Brie**)

Gorgonzola (perfect for the offspring of a family with "connections"...)

Gouda (will design desirable objects for the home)

Jarlsberg (gloomy Scandinavian detective with intuition and a drinking problem)

Manchego (rock idol with just the one name and millions of hysterical fans)

Monterey Jack (misbehavin' stockcar racin' teenage tearaway)

Mozzarella (*see* **Gorgonzola**)

Parmesan (international man of mystery)

Pecorino (an idle playboy who will probably marry **Gorgonzola**, cheat on her, and then die in a hail of bullets)

Ricotta (*see* **Gorgonzola**)

Roquefort (maybe a boxing champion?)

Samsø (brilliant blonde Danish detective with a personality disorder. A perfect partner for **Jarlsberg**)

Stilton (it's got authority; it's got class—the ideal choice for a lad with Presidential potential)

Fig. 40

A friendly heads-up for Pecorino from the in-laws

Cheesy Baby Names

Raising a Foodie

Raising little Langoustine to appreciate good food is something Mr. and Mrs. Foodie were both agreed upon from the very beginning. Weaned on puréed quails' breasts with spinach, used to puddings made with rare artisanal Madagascan chocolate, and with playmates picked from the foodie circle, not a morsel of fast food had passed the child's lips. She had mastered the fish soup/rouille/crouton/garlic/cheese routine by the time she was two; at three she could de-bone a sea bass; and was downing oysters and cracking crabs on her fourth birthday. Then came school.

With school came school lunch. With school lunch came the revelation of how good fat, sugar, and salt can taste, especially when coated in ersatz orange breadcrumbs and deep-fried in old lard. The consequence was tantrums and food wars, leaving poor little Langoustine (Tina to her friends) determinedly refusing her supper of daube de Provence with handmade noodles and wailing for fish sticks and oven chips.

Langoustine's parents have not given in—how could they? They'd never live it down if Langoustine were spotted emerging from KFC. So now she takes a lunchbox to school. Let's take a peek inside. She has a starter salad of baby salad leaves and Parmesan with roasted onions. That's lovely! Her main course is focaccia bread filled with homemade sun-dried tomatoes and slivers of chicken poached in stock and moistened with a mustardy mayonnaise. Irresistible! Her pudding is a tiny baked apple infused with calvados and filled with fat black raisins. For a snack, her papa has finely sliced a sweet potato, quickly fried the almost transparent slices, and seasoned them with smoked paprika. Yummy! Her new best friend Marlon unwraps his packed lunch: a packet of barbecue potato chips, a chocolate bar, and a tub of processed cheese (complete with strangely uniform orange breadsticks). Who ate what on this particular occasion I leave to your experience of how perverse a child can be. It should be noted that the foodie spent hours tempting his little Langoustine's palate back to the sunny, free-range upland pastures of wholesome wonderfulness. Marlon's mother spent about a minute casually destroying his.

Fig. 41

"Oooh yummy yummy! It's homard à la nage *for dinner!"*

Worship the Food

It's a broad church with welcoming arms and is so much more relevant to real life than most other belief systems. Say "no" to religions run by power-crazed, sexist despots and designed to cause stress, arguments, and wars! Worship The Food! This religion has everything a believer needs! Join now! Already there are temples built to worship The Food and shrines in every home. There are disciples who have interpreted The Food and written of their revelations in gospels. There is a reward and punishment system: heaven is experienced in an exquisite forkful of spaghetti with truffles and what passes for purgatory is a fast-food outlet in a windswept, out-of-town shopping mall. And hell? Hell is open to interpretation, but mouthfuls of warm gristle, emptying the dishwasher, and overcooked cabbage would get my vote.

As with any great religion, interpreting The Food has been fraught with dissent. Disciples did not speak with one voice about anything, which bought about "The Great Divide" that memorably split worshippers of The Food into warring "cuisines" very early on in the life of the church. Sad to say, added to these internal struggles, there were also forces of pure evil at work, determined to undermine all that The Food stood for with the creation of "nuggets" formed from strands of protein material and knitted together by machines, as well as drinks made from gas and sugar. Then the church's army of saints mounted a magnificent rescue job, with many attributing miracles to Escoffier, Marcella Hazan, Julia Child, Wolfgang Puck, Jamie Oliver, and (*insert your favorite here*).

Human nature being what it is, there have been schisms so deep that they have resulted in breakaway sects. (So, not very different from other religions after all.) Vegetarians turned their backs on many of the mainstream teachings of The Food in all its "Glorious Diversity," and went off on their own. It wasn't long before further splits occurred in that slightly anemic community as Vegans peeled off toward fanaticism and the Pescatorians desperately sought an excuse to eat fish.

Small groups of fanatics continue to gather around emerging charismatic leaders. Many claim that heavenly experiences are granted exclusively to those who invest in cast-iron range cookers or get their wives to build hay boxes. Others believe celebrity Science-ologists who claim we can only be saved by vaporized foam from another planet. What does The Food have to say about all this? It is difficult to speak for any god, but one imagines The Food is pleased to have so many devoted foodie followers blessed with common sense and a genuine love of The Food. They may dabble with heresy, but they will return to the fold.

Fig. 42

"Now don't take this too literally, Adam"

Foodie Movie Moments

Entirely subjective, and everyone has lists. So here's another one, proving that attitudes to food are a dead giveaway of character and a great way for a film-maker to describe relationships.

Character-revealing moments
- The scene from *Diary of a Mad Housewife* when Richard Benjamin, playing husband to said housewife, fixes a Cesar salad in the most pedantic way. You could so slap him.
- Danny DeVito in *Get Shorty*, doing the bossy "I'll order for you" routine in an LA restaurant and then ordering for himself an off-menu, egg-white omelet.
- Jack Nicholson's barely controlled sarcastic rage as he attempts to get plain toast with his omelet in *Five Easy Pieces*.
- Felix's ruined meatloaf dinner in *The Odd Couple*.
- Dance of the bread rolls in *The Gold Rush*. So poignant.

Things-bubbling-beneath-the-surface moments
- Tension-filled Thanksgiving dinners in *Brokeback Mountain* and excruciating family meals in *American Beauty*.

- Many films use the temptation of food as a metaphor for unlocking the uptight; *Babette's Feast* does it really well.

Knowing-your-place moments
- Snobbery personified in Maggie Smith's line about store-bought marmalade in *Gosford Park* and Paul Giamatti's line about refusing to lunch with people who drink Merlot in *Sideways*.

- Mealtimes as social minefield: there are many examples, but Julia Roberts in *Pretty Woman* did a pretty good job with the snail tongs.

Food-sex moments
- There are many, many examples of this, but the close-ups of Albert Finney and Joyce Redman lasciviously devouring chicken legs in *Tom Jones* set the standard back in 1963. At the other end of the scale, all those railway café lunches and cups of tea never touched by that heartbreakingly uptight, dutiful, never-to-be couple in *Brief Encounter*.

Murderous food moments
- All the *Godfather* movies had scenes of lavish, formal "family" banquets followed by gruesome killings.

- The bookend diner scenes in *Pulp Fiction* remind us that ruthless killers need comfort food.

And, in the Death-by-food category, the nominees are...
- Philippe Noiret in *La Grande Bouffe*, choking to death, his head nestled on a massive pair of pink blancmange breasts.
- The Fattest Man in the World, Mr. Creosote, exploding disgustingly in Monty Python's *The Meaning of Life* when finally defeated by that infamous wafer-thin mint.

Foodie Music

Here are some suggestions for a classic compilation for all your foodie friends. It will get them thinking about how food impacts life, love, and the waistband:

- *Memphis Soul Stew* (King Curtis) because it is a recipe: "Today's Special, of course, with half a tea cup of bass, a pound of fatback drums. Four teaspoons of boiling Memphis guitar, a little pinch of organ, half a pint of horns, place on the burner, and bring to a boil. Now. Beat. Well."

- *Sliced Tomatoes* (Just Brothers) and *Green Onions* (Booker T & the MG's) because they make a good salad and the onions keep the vampires away.

- *Do The Funky Chicken* (Rufus Thomas) to get people dancing round the kitchen.

- *Spanish Grease and Fried Neckbones And Some Home Fries* (Willie Bobo) to whet the appetite for satisfyin' heavy, greasy Latin food.

- *Guava Jelly* (Bob Marley), *Cream Puff* (Johnny Nash), and *Sugar, Sugar* (The Skatalites) for a touch of Caribbean flavor.

- *Bread And Butter* (The Newbeats): you know the writing's on the wall when the bread-and-butter lover finds his girl eating chicken dumplings with another man.

- *Watermelon Man* (Mongo Santamaria) and *Cantaloupe Island* (Herbie Hancock) for that refreshing melon moment.

- *Les Oignons* (Sidney Bechet), *Red Beans And Rice* (Louis Armstrong), *Red Onion Drag* (Louis Dumaine), and *Aubergines, Poivrons Et Sauce Tomate* (Sidney Bechet): the sort of songs you expect from New Orleans where the "musicianers" are as into their food as their music. How they love their veg!

- *Everybody Eats When They Come To My House* (Cab Calloway): an excuse to rhyme Hannah and Banana, Davy and Gravy, and so on.

- *Salt Peanuts* (Dizzy Gillespie and Charlie Parker) because it is such fun and an easy no-nonsense apéritif.

- *Gimme A Pigfoot And A Bottle Of Beer* (Bessie Smith): just to prove she ain't no stuck-up dame who drinks champagne and eats canapés.

- *Grits 'n' Greens* (Jimmy Neely): why does no one write about filet mignon and truffles?

- *Coleslaw* (Bill and Al Jennings): I know someone (now divorced and dropped off the radar) whose coleslaw made strong men trample over one another to get to the exit. Maybe Bill 'n' Al know her too.

Songs that are so obviously not about food...
- *All That Meat And No Potatoes* (Fats Waller)
- *Banana In Your Fruit Basket* (Bo Carter)
- *I Want A Little Sugar In My Bowl* (Nina Simone)
- *My Stove's In Good Condition* (Lil Johnson)
- *Get 'Em From The Peanut Man (Hot Nuts)* (Lil Johnson)

Well, time to stop all this nonsense because *My Pencil Won't Write No More* (Bo Carter).

Foodie Games

When the nights roll in, the washing up is done, the knives sharpened and oiled, seasonal shopping lists sorted, vegetable patch watered and weeded—the foodie's day is done and it's time to play!

Foodie scrabble: You can start by doubling word scores for a food-related word. Or ratchet up the pace by allowing foodie terms only. You will have to put aside the dictionary and agree on some sort of foodie bible as your arbitrating sourcebook. *Larousse Gastronomique* is as good as any. Try "Ziminu" on a triple word score. Since you ask, it is a *bouillabaisse* (fish stew) associated with Ajaccio in Corsica. Some useful short words: à and la.

Foodie consequences: A variation of the boy meets girl, somewhere, she says/he says, she does/he does, and the consequence game that you play with pencil and paper, folding over your contribution as you pass it round. In the foodie version it's: adjective, ingredient one; adjective, ingredient two; cooking method, with ingredient three; and they've named the dish...For example: Sour Pig's Bladder and Iced Pomegranates Steamed with Chocolate Buttons—and they named the dish "Hortense's Armpit." You get the drift.

Desert Island Dishes:You get to pick eight dishes that you could live on for the rest of your life. Plus one cookery book and one cooking implement. Variations include choosing one forever cuisine (mine would be Italian), one vegetable, one fruit (a tomato for me), and one type of meat or fish. Thought provoking.

Car-license-plate disgusting dishes: One for the road. Each player in turn spots a license plate and turns the letters into as disgusting a combination dish as they can. Rules are elastic but the letters must run in sequence and you have to describe your dish with relish. But please do make sure that the driver, when retching, does not take his or her eyes off the road. Take L945 ULE, for instance: you could go with Liquorice, Udder, and Lumpfish Parfait with Eels. Or Lamphries and Upside-down Cake with Larks in an Emmental Fondue.

Fig. 43

"Ooh, ohh, I've got a good one:
tiramisu with hummus, anchovies, and custard"

Going for a Walk—
Coming Back with Lunch

The countryside is so full of wondrous things to eat, and all for free! Bountiful nature has ensured that those of us bold enough to forage will never have to visit the supermarket ever again. Take a walk down a lane with an enthusiastic forager foodie and you'll come back with an overflowing basketful of blackberries, brambleberries, sloes, crab apples, hedge garlic, sorrel, wild mushrooms, and nettles. *Sooo* tasty! Do think of the fruity pies, the delicate jellies, and the robust soups. Don't think of the terrible mistakes you could be making with fatal fungi, deadly berries, and pointless mouthfuls of grass.

So, what else do country roads have to offer? Anyone for a tasty casserole of squashed hedgehog or a fox-cub fricassée? I didn't think so. What else has the foraging foodie got in the freezer? Bats, weasels, cats, squirrels, and a tasty toad scraped from the tarmac or perhaps pheasants and hares found dead in the hedgerows? How nice. Some nicer than others.

High time for practical advice from the foraging fraternity that I am happy to pass on: do cook your roadkill well. Apparently, if the squashed animal has been dead a while and turned green, it may taste a little bland but it can still be eaten if well butchered and well cooked. In general, fresh, identifiable roadkill despatched with a glancing blow of the front bumper is considered superior to the "guess-that-mess" with a tire track design.

As it says on the menu of the Road Kill Café:

Eating food is more fun
When you know it was hit on the run.

Fig. 44

Braised with a bunch of nettles for three hours or so, it'll be lovely!

Don't Get
Too Fond of Flopsy

Once upon a time, children, there was this lovely garden full
of happy animals. It was, I suppose, a bit like a petting zoo.
Chickens squawked and scrabbled around in the open air, ducks
and geese ducked and dived for weedy algae in the pond, rabbits
snuffled adorably in their nice clean hutches, guinea pigs
likewise, and maybe there was a family of little pigs playing
in the mud—but does that give the game away?

At feeding time, the nice lady who owns the garden appeared
with various buckets, chuntering in a friendly, reassuring way
to the animals, handing out fresh greens to Flopsy and Mopsy,
scattering corn for Jemima and her feathered friends, and gaily
filling the swill bins for the little piggies. Aaahhh!

But this is no pet paradise, children, and if you can't take the
consequences of sustainable living, then stop reading at once
and hand this book immediately to a cynical adult. For this is the
gingerbread cottage of your nightmares, girls and boys. This is
where the foraging foodie (not unlike the witch who fattened up
Hansel and Gretel) is trying to figure out who is ready for the pot.

A handy tip: rabbits are best killed with a sudden blow behind
the ears with a heavy stick and then skinned while still warm.

A tasty recipe: guinea pig is delicious flattened out and pan-fried
with bacon.

Sleep tight, children. Sweet dreams!

Fig. 45

The day started out uneventfully…

Don't Get Too Fond of Flopsy

Index

Aga, the 28–9
anchovies 50
animals
  for adventurous
    eating 94–5
  edible pets 124
  intimate parts of
    42
  roadkill 122
appliances,
  electrical 66–7
authentic ethnic
  food 96–7

baby names, for
  foodies 104–8
baby vegetables 40
baked beans 50
balsamic vinegar 58
beach barbecue 32–3
beans, canned 50
Black Forest
  gateau 18, 19
blog, foodie's
  88–90
blowtorches 24–5
books, for foodies
  100–1
bread 48

canned foods 50
car-license-plate
  disgusting dishes
    121
cheeses
  as baby names
    109–11

themed 30–1
chemistry set
  cooking 26–7
children
  food for 112–13
  and pets 124
chilies, speciality
  hot 52
Christmas 36–7
coffee, equipment
  for making 54
competitive dining
  6–8
Consequences,
  foodie 120
convenience foods,
  canned 50
cookbooks, novels
  as 100–1
country life
  and the Aga 28–9
  roadkill 122–3
country of origin,
  cheeses 30–1
cutlery 12–13

desert island
  dishes 120
dissenters 114–15
dry ice 26

ethnic food 96–7

facts, too many 22,
  80–1
films, movie
  moments 116–17

fish, unfamiliar 44
fishcakes,
  deconstructed
    91–2
food
  obscure provenance
    22, 30, 60, 64
  as religion 114–15
foodies
  baby names for
    104–8, 109–10
  as critic (blog)
    88–90
  dreams of 91–3
  gifts for 68–9
  novels for 100–1
  recommendations
    from menu 84–7
  as regular
    customer 82–3
fork, battery-powered
  spaghetti 13
France, myths 102
fugu (Japanese
  blowfish) 44–5

gadgets 24–5
games, foodie 120–1
gifts, for foodies
  68–9
goose, for
  Christmas 36–7
guts 'n' gore, bits of
  animals 42

holiday destinations,
markets 76–7
hosts, absent 20–1

information, too
much 22, 80–1
irony food 18–19

Japanese blowfish
44–5
Johnson, Hugh 72

knives, kitchen 66–7

malt vinegar 58
markets, abroad 76–7
Masters of Wine
74–5
meat(s)
exotic 94–5
gruesome bits 42
menus
the foodie
recommends 84–7
lovingly hand-
written 80–1
molecular
gastronomy 26–7
movie moments
116–17
music, foodie
118–19
myths 102–3

novels, for foodies
100–1

olive oil 60–1
olives, pretentious 22
organic foods, myth
102

ortolan, myth 102–3
oysters, myth 102

pets, edible 124
picnics 34–5, 100
plates, strangely-
shaped 14–15

rabbits 124
religion of foodies
114–15
restaurant critic,
foodie's blog 88–90
restaurants
foodie's ambitions
for 91–2
menus 80–1, 84–7
the regular foodie
customer 82–3
three-star dining
78–9
roadkill 122–3

salads
competitive 16–17
main-course 17
salt 64–5
school lunches
112–13
scientific
ingredients 26–7
Scrabble, foodie 120
seafood cocktail
18–19
seasonal food 46–7
seaweed 33
spinach, iron in 103
steak, with
mushrooms 19
sun-dried tomatoes
62

tables
laying 13
over-decorated
6–8
tea 56–7
tomatoes, sun-dried
62
tools, heavyweight
24–5
truffle shaver 66

utensils, specialist
66–7

vegans 115
vegetables
invisible 8
miniature baby
40–1
vegetarians 115
vinegar 58

wild food 122
wines
from obscure
locations 72–3
language of 74–5

Acknowledgments

I would like to thank the following:

My editor, Pete Jorgensen, whose idea this book was, for having the foresight to commission me to write it and for making the whole process so enjoyable.

My husband, Iain Parsons, for laughing at my jokes and contributing so many of his own.

The illustrator, Steve Millington, for adding his own delightful spin.